WHAT COLOR
IS MY RIBBON?

WHAT COLOR IS MY RIBBON?

Carole McCaskill

To order additional copies of this book, contact:
Xlibris Corporation
1-888-795-4274
www.Xlibris.com
Orders@Xlibris.com
56785

This book is dedicated to my loves Dan and Josh. You make life what it is, joyous. Daily, I give thanks that you are my family.

It is also dedicated to my extended family and friends. Without my wonderful support network this journey would have been difficult and this book would have been impossible.

I must also dedicate this book to all the strangers and acquaintances that through circumstance now fill the pages of this book. You may recognize yourself on one of these pages, and think . . . "I may have seen her typing away feverishly on her blackberry!"

Table of Contents

Introduction

Hi Guys,

Forest Gump said, "Life is like a box of chocolates" ~~well I think~~ friends are like a ~~box of chocolates.~~ Inside each one of them is ~~something~~ different, delicious, and on any given day, there's one with a wonderful filling inside that when consumed, satisfies the soul. That's the beauty of having a whole box . . . each one is appreciated for its uniqueness!

Love to all of you,

Carole

This book is a collection of letters – alright emails – nobody writes letters these days, except my mother. I began writing these emails because I realized how concerned my friends and family were, about my diagnosis of ovarian cancer, and I knew that if they were sad and worried, I would be too and I knew I needed to be positive and happy as I went on this journey.

I think all of us have our roles in life that also vary from situation to situation. My role, with my friends is two-fold; first I am one of the organizers. I tend to organize lots of activities, parties etc. My other role is that of the logical, solution finder with just the right answers. Now where do I turn for answers? Typically I help myself. So these emails are a result of my cancer, while trying to help myself. This book is a result of the response to my emails with more and more friends saying how much they looked forward to these emails, how positive I was and asking permission if they can pass them on to other friends.

9

So in my typical role of the "solution finder", I hope that this book can help those with cancer find humor and an understanding of the power of a positive attitude in their quest to prevail. For anyone else reading this, that they too can find that a positive attitude can help you feel in control of your life, empowered and find joy in everything you do.

This email collection has been dubbed my "Hi Guys" emails . . . I use "guys" to mean both males and females and so that is how most of these emails start. My "Guys" actually constitute a collection of people that range from my nearest and dearest girlfriends, my immediate and extended family, co-workers and acquaintances that care. Throughout this book you will be introduced to many of these "Guys". Some of these emails are sent to specific people and some are email responses to the mails I sent out. I received so many supportive emails back that I simply could not include all of them. If you want to know more about my "Guys", I have included a short, funny story, about how each of these people fit into my life, at the back of the book. Thanks again to all of you for taking part in my "Living Journal," a journal that responds back!

Some emails are short. Some are long. Some are funny. Some are informative and some comforting to those around me and some I hope are insightful. In all, I hope that you enjoy reading this collection of emails. I have tried to find humor in a very devastating, world affecting disease.

Listen to the Whispers

These emails were exchanged PRIOR to and leading up to my diagnosis. I wanted to add these to the book so you can see how the symptoms were there, but could be missed or can be mistaken for other less serious issues. As Ovarian Cancer Canada tries to teach . . ."Listen to the Whispers"!

July 16, 2007
Subject: Off I go!

Hi Cathy,

Cedar Point is great. Earlier I was waiting for everyone to get off a roller coaster . . . I just went on two low ones (height issues) I screamed so much I peed I bit. LOL. I'm used to going to the bathroom often – now I have to go immediately. I'll have to do some Kegels! He-He. Maybe its time for Depends!

See you!

Carole

July 18, 2007

Hi Cathy,

I got my period . . . never fun when you are camping . . . in a tent and your body is insisting on waking you up twice a night to go for a pee! My period seems to be heavier than normal! Oh well the campsite is beautiful!

See ya soon,

Carole

July 25, 2007

Hey MJ,

Remember I had my annual last month and just thought I should get checked for ovarian cancer. No real reason, except that I might be at higher risk. I got the results from my trans-vaginal ultrasound - Good news it came back negative! The technician was a bit pissed off at me since she said my bladder wasn't full. It seemed full to me. LOL, I guess that's why I pee so often!

See you at golf after work. Are Vicki and Sandra joining us? Kay can't make it but if Peggy is playing we will need two tee times.

Call me,

Carole

August 4, 2007

Hi Cathy,

I can't believe I got my period again. So much for my 28 day cycle, 3 days of light bleeding - welcome to peri-menopause. Perhaps it is camping and the full moon. Lots of laundry to do when we get home! I hope I have enough supplies!

Are you still waiting for yours? How many days now? 35?

See you later,

Carole

August 31, 2007

Hi Gwen,

Don't mention this, but on Tuesday I have to lay off 2 women that work for me. My stomach feels terrible. My stomach is literally turning. It's bad enough having to do it, but on the first day back to school! Of course I always worry if I will get laid off after I have done the dirty deed. I don't think so but I always wonder. This period is so heavy. I am bleeding like a stuck pig. I am sure it is the stress.

Carole

September 4, 2007

Hi Guys,

I cried. They cried. It was tough. I now have to fill in for both of them. Plus I wonder about my counterpart in Phoenix. He seems great, but is there a plan to get rid of one of us? Looking forward to starting yoga! A little pain in my lower abdomen! Not enough to really worry about. It must be this heavy period!

See you at coffee tomorrow,

Carole

September 10, 2007

Hi Judy,

My belly is a still little sore and I had trouble keeping up with the boys on our after lunch walk. The worse part is I seem to go to the bathroom so much. I feel constipated but then I am loose. Sorry I know this is gross but I have to bitch to someone.

Thanks for listening!

Carole

September 17, 2007

Hi Sonya,

I went to the doctor at work after lunch. I'm now getting cramps
and I get bloated after eating. Do you think its IBS or just all
this stress? I am so busy filling in for the two positions . . .
and we have this big project with Phoenix. I'll have to look up
these symptoms, in my symptoms book.

The doctor gave me a prescription and set me up for an ultrasound
but it isn't until Oct. 1.

Carole

September 18, 2007

Hi Cathy,

Did Brian tell you about who we met at the coffee club this morning?
Ivan. She's a writer who is staying in the provincial park. I bought
a copy of her book, very intriguing. I told Dan about her. I hope
she is at coffee Saturday morning so Dan gets to meet her.

Carole

September 21, 2007

Hi Sally,

Okay so now I am starting to worry. After a two day liquid diet I
am still bloated, constipated alternating with diarrhea! Severe
cramping, I am so stressed at work. I think I have developed IBS.
I am going to Phoenix next week. Aside from getting up to speed
faster on this project with the team down there, I am hoping
that meeting them will make me feel less vulnerable. I am still
feeling like I could get the axe . . . . I think it is just my stupid
hormones shifting. I never worry like this. I keep getting a real
gut wrenching feeling. My stomach literally seems to drop!

Carole

September 23, 2007

Hi Patrick and Tim,

Thanks for dinner last night. We enjoyed it. Sorry I couldn't eat.
I was full after just eating the soup, which was delicious. We'll
have you guys over for dinner when I get back from Phoenix.

Carole

September 24, 2007

Hi Cathy,

On my way to Phoenix! On a stopover in Philly! Thank goodness
for my blackberry! Josh will be happy I got him a ton of Eagles
stuff for his birthday. Speaking of which, Sonya is having her
birthday party Fri night. She invited Brian at the coffee club
this morning but he said he is working his night shift that night,
so I thought I'd mention it to you in case he forgets to mention
it to you.

Have fun at yoga tonight - practice that downward dog!
By the way, I'm glad your wait is over;-) What was it 45 days???
I'll probably get my period again . . . I think I'd rather be on
the "not getting my period so much" end of this!
Hope to get my stomach sorted out soon - it is starting to "cramp"
my style LOL!

See you later,

Carole

September 25, 2007

Hi Cathy,

We are going to Deb and Rheal's party on Friday, I forgot. I think
Sonya will change her party to another night. How long we stay
will depend on my stomach. Yesterday was one of the worse days.
Hope today is better.

Email you after my shower! Its only 6:15 with the time change and
I am wide-awake. I needed to sleep with a hot water bottle and I
am taking Pepto-Bismol and Tylenol . . . At least the temperature
is 95 – Phoenix is always nice.

Carole

September 27, 2007

Hi Cathy,

On my way home – in Philly again! I called the Mitel nurse from
the airport in Phoenix to see if I should go to the hospital in
Phoenix. I decided to get home first . . . saves on all the hassle
with insurance and I would feel stupid if this is just IBS.

I've been sitting on the tarmac in Philly for an hour and a half.
My stomach is dying. I may go to the ER tomorrow. It's bloated and
hard all the time now. Just needed to bitch so I don't scream!
See you tomorrow,

Carole

September 27, 2007

Hi Dan,

Going on hour 3, on the tarmac!

I was supposed to be home by now. Bad weather on the east coast
has caused the delay . . . Some idiot got up and went to the
bathroom without checking with the stewardess and we missed our
spot in the queue to take off! We now have to go back to the
terminal because we ran out of "taxiing fuel"! Got to go. Need to
rebook a flight. I'm going to call from my blackberry while still
on the plane. They won't even rebook us.

Love you, bye.

Carole

September 27, 2007

Hi Hon,

Got a flight but – I don't have a seat yet. If I don't get on this flight I may need to go to emergency here in Philly.

Carole

Septembre 27, 2007

Hi Hon,

I am now on my second plane. The asshole from the other plane that got up to go for a pee while we were waiting in line to take off without checking with the stewardess – causing us to lose our spot in line on the runway – causing us to run out of fuel – causing the flight cancellation, is now sitting behind me. He was on standby on this flight, weaseled his way onto this flight ahead of me – when I wasn't on standby! Now he just told the stewardess he's diabetic and needs food, got someone to get him food from inside the airport – said to get any sandwich and any drink, which a diabetic wouldn't do. Such an ass wipe! I just want to yell at him.

Love you,

Carole

September 27, 2007

Hi Hon,

I CANNOT believe this!!! So they accepted about half of my old flight onto this flight. We are all seated. And now they are asking for some passenger, some guy, to get off the flight! Nobody will admit that's who they are!!! The Stewardess is now checking all the men's passports – to get the guy off the plane. He doesn't want to get off. Tim, the guy from work I am travelling with – they asked him to get off . . . even though it isn't him that they are looking for . . . the guy that was the last in the standby queue. They found the guy and made him get off the plane. Idiot passenger number 2!

Maybe we can leave now!

September 27, 2007

Hi Hon,

You'll never believe this! After leaving the terminal we had to return again . . . because idiot passenger number 2's luggage didn't get taken off!!!!

Will I ever get home :-(
Love you . . .

Carole

September 27, 2007

Hi Hon,

Looks like I won't land in Ottawa until 2am – I have been on the tarmac since 4pm!!! I can't even bend over in my cramped seat to pick up my purse. I was going to go to emergency tonight but I guess I will have to go tomorrow. It's even a little hard to breath now . . . not to bad – just can't take a deep breath my abdomen is so distended. I started to tear up. The nice French lady beside said "Don't worry we'll be home soon" . . . I just managed to get out "It's not that. I need to go to emergency!" See you at 3am . . .

Love you,

Carole

The Journey Begins

September 28, 2007

I go to the ER. After giving the triage nurse my symptoms, she states that I probably could have "waited until Monday for my previously scheduled ultrasound appointment at the clinic." I get in unusually quickly. This is at 10:30 in the morning. I am very uncomfortable and have developed a cough. The nurses keep asking me if I want morphine. It makes me puke, so I decline. Besides, I hate being "hazy".

After an initial visit with the doctor and drawing blood, I am told they want to give me a trans-vaginal ultrasound. Although I had just had one two months earlier – this seems like a reasonable course of action.

With Dan at my side, waiting for the test, we discuss the possibility of an ectopic pregnancy – not unfounded considering my knowledge of the adhesions that encase my right fallopian tube that had made pregnancy a miracle of modern science for me. Then it hit. My period. Ah, not a pregnancy, wait, perhaps it still could be, an ectopic pregnancy. Bleeding would still fit that self-diagnosis!

As soon as I saw the ultrasound screen I saw some weird things. (No I am not an ultrasound technician – let me digress, when I was pregnant with twins, I had what is called twin to twin transfusion. In a nutshell, I had an ultrasound twice a week from 3 months into my pregnancy until I gave birth to Josh, a preemie, at 6 months gestation. So I really saw a ton of ultrasounds – at least of my abdomen . . . .) So when I saw a tubular shaped shadow . . .

I suspected . . . well the first thing I thought was . . . did I
take my tampon out? Oh no how embarrassing . . . but I had, so
what was this strange shaped "thing" in my abdomen . . . it all
was very strange and the shadows seemed "cloudy". Later, I learned
that it was fluid in my abdomen and the tube shaped 'thing' was
a tumor.

Then came a chest X-Ray, considering that breathing deeply had
become hard in the last week, it seemed appropriate, which was
followed by a CAT scan. This was entirely new to me and unfortunately
there was no monitor to peer into my insides . . . my curiosity
was overwhelming! I hate having no control . . .

Dan and I decided that he should go pick up our 12 year old son
and bring him to the hospital. As I was waiting to see what was
next, half clothed and dangerously close to being at the end of
my magazine collection, that Dan had bought for me to pass the
time away, I saw John from Fitzroy Harbour, where I live. What an
unusual conversation, "Ya they're doing tests . . . don't know,
but my stomach aches . . . see you around". While waiting, I
heard a conversation between two nurses " . . . no wonder she's
uncomfortable . . . isn't she on morphine?" I wondered if it was
me that they were discussing . . .

After a trans-vaginal ultrasound, chest X-Ray and a CAT scan and
after Dan spending 8 hours with me at the hospital, the doctor
delivers the diagnosis, while I am alone. Ovarian cancer. I can
feel the blood rush from me. My immediate reaction is "Can you
take it out right now?" "No." "Okay." Then it is a blur. I picked
my blackberry and delivered the most devastating news anybody
can deliver, on my blackberry to Dan . . . "Come quick!" . . .
and then tears.

When Josh and Dan arrived, we told my son. I was in tears. He was
scared. What else can you do? In all the conversations I have had
in my head. This was never one of them. I, like so many others,
never really felt that I would get cancer . . . at least not at
45 . . . well 46 minus two weeks.

What a shock . . . especially after receiving a negative test
result for ovarian cancer on a trans-vaginal ultrasound less than

2 months earlier! By 7 pm that night. My life had changed forever. One week earlier I was concerned over two conflicting parties that were booked for this night.

As Dan and I drive to my mother's house to deliver the news, I told him "I don't know how to be." This is something I will need to figure out! Who do you tell? How do you tell them? When do you tell them? How do you do it without bringing everyone down? This is new to me. I will definitely need to figure out "how to be."

When I look back on all the "whispers", all the clues . . . I see that they all fit. I also see though that most of these symptoms can be confused with many other problems. We all need to listen to the whispers and when you feel that something is not right – keep pushing. I am like that – I guess ovarian cancer truly sneaks up on you. It is most likely that my first ultrasound was a false negative, or perhaps it was missed. At this juncture the point is moot. Nothing will change unless I missed the news that a time machine has already been invented.

Hint you can use – a hospital may be a better place to get this type of ultrasound. Another tip you can use – If you are at higher risk of ovarian cancer, know about the CA125 blood test. It is a marker for ovarian cancer. This test can result in a false positive, but I would imagine coupled with a follow up of a trans-vaginal ultrasound – it might be worth the $35.00, which is what you get charged in Ontario as it is currently not covered by OHIP.

September 29, 2007
Subject: Taking control

Yesterday, I was diagnosed with ovarian cancer. Even with this diagnosis, I realized that I wanted to take control, and ensure I made the best of the situation. I strongly believe in a few basic principles:

1. You can't wait for fun, you have to make fun wherever and whenever you can.
2. Truly being happy is a sum of all the small moments in your life . . . not the big events.
3. You only get one chance at your life - YOU must make sure you have the life you want.

I have already heard from more and more friends, co-workers past and present and general well wishers. The more things are becoming clear, the more I can see the connectedness between us all, and our dependence on each other's strengths and weaknesses. I just received an email from an old work friend named John, that I have known for 20 years, who recently retired. In his email he reminded me of my strength but more importantly he reminded me that I am a linear thinker. This has been one of my best assets at my job in high tech, but it is my weakness when it comes to writing down my thoughts. It is very hard for me to just "go". I need to know where I am going and how I am getting there. Couple this revelation, with advice from my new found friend of three weeks, Ivan, who happens to be a published writer, with whom I had discussed getting started writing a book prior to hearing about my cancer and her giving me the same advice from a different perspective. "Just start writing. You can edit and organize later." Basically she taught me in that one quick statement, that I have to let the creativity flow. This paragraph is my stream of consciousness at this moment . . . it seems unorganized, it is begging for order and I am resisting. Writing has always allowed me to feel a modicum of control when clearly what is happening in my life right now is beyond my control . . . we will see where this journey takes us! And Now I begin to write!

September 30, 2007

I am back at the ER, this time with a scheduled visit, for them
to drain the accumulated fluid in my abdomen. I am told this will
help me to eat and breathe better. They give me a local, and with
a very small tool (it looks like a laparoscopy tool I had in an
earlier "procedure") they then proceed to drain 4 liters of a
yellowish fluid (it reminds me of a low grade engine oil) Here's
a good comparison - 4 liters, that's like delivering a 10 pound
baby! No wonder I couldn't breathe, and my pants didn't fit. Ahhh,
this is a new experience for me . . . Josh, only weighed 3.2 oz
when I delivered him. So this is what pregnant women complain
about!

They also take a sample tissue from my omentum. That is the fat
that is deep in your belly. No amount of sit-ups will change
this . . . apparently it protects our lower abdomen . . . humm
is it the 'deep fat' tissue they talk about being bad for you or
is it, yet another layer of fat we have to worry about? Do men
have this too or can we women blame our middle age bellies on our
'big omentum' - kinda like being big boned?

Oh if I were vindictive . . . I would have loved to tell the
triage nurse what my diagnosis was! But I'm not. So I didn't. I
wonder how many times ovarian cancer gets diagnosed in emergency
rooms across the country? It takes a lot to get me to go to the
emergency room - the last time was when I broke my back in a car
accident 25 years ago. I think I have been to the ER four times
in my life. First was for a broken arm in Grade 6, second was my
first year in college . . . pain in my abdomen with a slightly high
white count . . . not high enough for an appendicitis attack . . .
but was diagnosed as a "spastic duodenum" (a valve between your
stomach and intestinal track - which I think they now call
Irritable Bowel Syndrome! This is why I thought that this could
be my problem now.) Now, ovarian cancer! Definitely a called for
trip to the ER. Better than waiting a week to get results back
from a clinic and more testing to discover this! I think this
visit to emergency is a good thing, I found out sooner. I bet I
saved a few weeks or maybe even a month . . . so this is a good
thing . . . well you know what I mean.

Living Journal

October 1, 2007
Subject: Push . . . nicely

Hi Guys,

Thanks for all your emails. I thought I would send one big one to all of you.

Dan is busy scurrying around! Sue (you know my neighbor as a kid . . . who comes out for Boxing Day brunch every year . . .) she's a nurse and I called her right away. Sue connected me with someone who has ovarian cancer. She told me all the tests and things that we need to try to rush our way through the early stages of getting into the cancer center. She said, "I need to go to the Shirley Greenberg Center at the Riverside Hospital", apparently that's where all the women's cancer intake happens prior to going to the cancer center at the General. Officially I don't have cancer until the oncologist confirms it! She seems a bit pessimistic but I am grateful for her help . . . Let me know if I get pessimistic okay ladies! Oh ya, she tells me that I want to get Dr. Fung Ke Fung as my Oncologist . . . he's the best. Sounds like a disco band to me!

Dan has spent the last several days trying to jumpstart the process. You know how sometimes Dan is such a "chatty Cathy" talking to anyone and everyone (which is sometimes a bit embarrassing but is great for this situation!!!) I am so glad of it now. He has had great success opening doors to get things going. He went

27

back to the Queensway Carleton Hospital to get a copy of my CAT scan. Mary still works there and helped us get a disk of the CAT scan. Apparently I need it. (Potentially one visit saved!) He got copies of all the blood work and other tests. I looked at some of the blood test results – lots of the measurements were way out of whack but darned if I know what they all mean!

Dan managed to get into see a nurse at both the Riverside Hospital, and at the cancer center at the General Hospital. I think we have all our information ready to go. We still need a CA 125 blood test. Something that confirms ovarian cancer! Dan asked the doctor at Mitel (my place of work) to write up an order to get one. She did. She wrote up a referral to get into the oncologist. This is a bonus since I went in through emergency . . . but I need a GP or a referral from someone to get into the oncologist. I got one. The blood test is $35. A case of beer . . . done!

Carole

October 2, 2007
Subject: A 34 year hiatus.

Hi Guys,

I guess the time is now. The idea of writing a book has been whirling around in my head for many years. Until now I had always felt my life was too boring to write about and I didn't feel I could piece together a fiction work that could hold a reader's attention . . . And now either by grand design, fate or destiny, I have some time and something to write about. I guess I should have paid attention to the idiom "Be careful what you wish for . . ."

So here I am. I have just been diagnosed with ovarian cancer. Which although on the surface is of considerable concern, I have chosen to look at it as a kick in the butt, a reminder to do what I have been putting off doing for far too long.

It is day one of putting pen to paper. My birthday is in 6 days. I will be 46. My first attempt at writing came when I was just 10. I started a novel. I wrote about 20 pages of words about my life with my girlfriends in grade 6. My spelling was atrocious, but my vocabulary wasn't bad – I'll chalk that up to *Nancy Drew*, *The Bobbsy Twins* and other novels that captured my imagination and always had me reading long past my bedtime, under my covers with a flashlight.

I suppose my reaction to the news of ovarian cancer is not necessarily typical but it certainly was a wake up call for me. Three nights ago – after just hearing the news, I found myself slipping into the bathroom in the middle of the night, writing down my feelings, thoughts and an opening for this book. Of course I had the normal reaction – your typical – questions when hearing devastating news about your health. But what surprised me was the stress I felt because I had not accomplished my goal of writing.

Carole

October 3, 2007
Subject line: dark and wandering writings, the
search and finding my way . . .

Hi Guys,

My thoughts about this book were heading off in the philosophical, metaphysical and religious direction. This is not necessarily where I had intended it to go. However it does not surprise me as this has been occupying a large portion of my thoughts lately. I still don't know what I want out of this. I think I want someway of telling my son all of this. Telling him truly who I am, what I think and what is important to me. I want to help direct his life in a direction that will resonate well within him. I want his happiness. Happiness is comfort, it is a state of being, which brushes up against optimism and confidence and finds its way in love and self-actualization. This is where I will take my thoughts . . .

Happiness comes from sitting on your front porch on a mid Oct. day in Ottawa – simply because it is warm enough. With the sun shinning and finding peace in the incessant humming of the bumblebee that should have been asleep weeks before and knowing that without the bee's humming you would not be outside enjoying such a glorious fall day.

Happiness is, knowing that as you look at all the wonders of nature around you, the birds, and the changing leaves, the fall mums, and yes, even the dying annuals hanging from summer baskets. It is also an understanding that we have been charged with protecting what we are destroying. We must use our gift of reason wisely.

As I take deep breaths, in an effort to kill the cancer cells growing within me I know that there is a force or energy that connects us all and as I breathe – I know that I am one with nature. I let the universe know my intention. "I will beat this cancer." I breathe in and feel the air killing the anaerobic cancer cells . . . my life is changing as I write. I embrace the change and all the new challenges and beauty that will come with it. Breathe. It is wondrous! Open your eyes wide, smile and look at a tree, a flower, a bee, they know their purpose. Discover yours. Breathe.

I shall find where this writing will take me . . .

Carole

October 3, 2007
Subject: Thank your Aunt!

Hi Cathy,

I wanted to thank you so much for the information about the "cancer diet" . . . well the diet that helps beat cancer . . . the diet that works with chemo – not against it . . . anyway – the diet! Not only am I trying to eat what's on the diet, I went to the web page and it has catapulted me to an extensive on-line search into antioxidants, healthy options, chemicals, etc. etc. I am so glad to hear that someone with stage 4 cancer is having such great success with lifestyle changes. It gives me great hope and my on-line searching occupies my time and feels empowering with all that I am learning.

Thanks,
Carole

October 4, 2007
Subject: Breathe easier

Hi Guys,

Since my diagnosis, we have had our vents cleaned; we got a HEPA air filter to help me breathe easier. And yet, only today's visit has made me breathe easier. Without either of us discussing it, while purposely avoiding reading about stages and associated prognosis, we hoped for some good news.

We have come into this doctor's visit armed with records, CAT scans, X-rays and a CA125 blood test. After the nurse takes a brief history, Dr. Le (not doctor Fung Ke Fung) performs a test where two fingers are inserted into two orifices at the same time. I'll let your imagination tell you which ones. I scream. Let me put it to you this way. My C-Section pain was an 8 out of 10. My abdomen for the past two weeks has been a 5 out of 10. This was an 11! He confirms that it appears I have cancer. He then tells me that they did not receive the fluid analysis nor biopsy results from the Queensway Carleton Hospital. I am told the hospital says they didn't do a biopsy but only siphoned off the fluid from my abdomen. They tell me that I will need to come back.

"No!!!" I yell in my head, "I can't handle another week. I need to get things rolling!"

I describe the procedure and point to the small mark on my abdomen where they took the biopsy and the other mark on my abdomen where they drained the fluid. The nurse says, "Ya that's exactly what the procedure is . . ." She leaves the room. The doctor finished the exam, which includes listening to my lungs. We are just about to leave and the nurse comes back. She has the fluid results. No biopsy but the fluid is enough for Dr. Le. He tells me. Stage 3. Dan and I are alone in the exam room. We both sigh. We both are happy it is not stage 4. (That was the first and last time we ever discuss my stage.) We did not ask for a prognosis. We are just happy. We breathe easier.

I get home and symbolically turn off the HEPA Filter system . . . in fact my breathing has returned to normal now that there is not 4 liters of fluid pressing on my lungs. I have an appointment set at the Cancer Center next week.

Carole

October 6, 2007
Subject: Sigh

Hi Guys,

Today is Josh's birthday . . . He is having a party. For the first time in my life I am missing his birthday party. I am at home alone. Stretched out, trying to breathe, trying to relax my abdomen! It is just too tough to even write.

Carole

October 8, 2007
Subject: Another Sigh

Hi Guys,

Today is my birthday and Thanksgiving. Dan, Josh and I are at my parents' house. I smile but I am sad. I put on a brave face I don't want people sad. I can't even eat mashed potatoes and gravy (I am learning what to eat to help beat cancer . . .) A full Thanksgiving dinner is not on the list! I am eating other vegetables and a bit of Turkey. No wine . . . that's a hard one!

Carole

October 10, 2007
Subject: What color is my ribbon?

Hi Guys,

It has become my tradition to buy a small token Christmas gift that supports breast cancer, for all the women in my family. Last year they received pretty little notebooks sporting a pink ribbon, generously sold in support of breast cancer by Avon. The year before was the "thing me boob" key chains/purse adornments put out by the Canadian Cancer Society. This year they will receive fanny packs (sorry Brits-that's what we call them . . . butt bags to you) . . . you know those pouches that go around your waist to carry change etc. – again with the highly recognizable pink ribbon on it. With my "thing me boob" attached to my purse I looked at my Oncologist's nurse last week and jokingly said "I guess I have been supporting the wrong cancer all these years." Of course I was joking and I am glad to support such a good cause.

As it turns out, October is Breast Cancer Awareness month. Now on short-term disability, from my job in high tech, I do what any self-respecting working women does when she has time off – I turned on Oprah, Ellen, The Tyra Banks Show and the View, and got caught up on all the talk shows. It seems that every second show has topics relating to breast cancer. I am inspired by Melissa Etheridge's story about beating breast cancer and am pleased to hear that she too felt that it was a journey and awakening of her spirituality, and an understanding of where she fits in unison with the world and how the planet and we are all connected. But I also wonder, where is the awareness for ovarian cancer? What color is my ribbon?

I have become aware of the fact that I cannot name one famous person who has suffered from ovarian cancer. Where is our spokesperson? I cannot think of one company on the TSE or Dow Jones that sponsors ovarian cancer. Is it taboo? Is it our North American aversion to sex or sexual discussion in general that leads to this? Or is it just the fact that nobody has taken the time to get things started? If that is the case, then consider it started!
What color is my ribbon?

Do I need to tell you how terrible cancer is? No – we all know. One in three people will be diagnosed with cancer. Soon to be one in two! Do I need to tell you how terrible ovarian cancer is? No – all cancer is bad. What I do need to tell you is that there is a simple blood test that detects symptoms of ovarian cancer. The CA125 blood test. A simple blood test! Why is this simple blood test not a part of our yearly physical exam? In Ontario it costs $35. You can ask your doctor for one. It's not covered by

OHIP but it's not even mentioned! Give women a choice to pay for one! What color is my ribbon?

I hope that I can engage enough women with this book to have them at least take a minute, to find out the symptoms. Ask a few questions. Well what color is my ribbon? I have never seen one but I do have a ribbon. It is my pledge to make my ribbon come out from obscurity and at least take second place behind the pink ribbon – we have all come to recognize and support!

Carole

October 11, 2007
Subject: a window has closed . . . and a door has opened

Hi Guys,

Tomorrow my life truly changes forever. Tomorrow I have my first visit in my journey to recovery. Over the past week I have changed my diet, I have eliminated many toxins, and many of the trappings associated with our commercialized environment. I am no longer consuming any processed foods. I am eating mostly vegetables, beans, and small amounts of protein. I am not eating sodium, no sugar, no fats, few carbohydrates, no dairy except for yogurt and quark. I am eating wheat grass, sheep sorrel and other things I have never heard of, nor contemplated eating a week ago! I have lost weight, but I am eating avocadoes and whey powder, I am drinking lots of water, green tea and herbal teas. I am trying to balance this "cancer diet" with maintaining my weight.

Tomorrow it all changes! Tomorrow I am told my course of treatment. At least this is what I believe. I hope for the best, but prepare for the worst. I am ready to fight for it all. My acorn is just about to grow into something grand. This I know.

Carole

October 12, 2007
Subject: I'm in the system

Hi Guys,

So Dan and I went to the first my first appointment at the cancer
center today. It was so packed. They were on time though. That's
always a bonus. Today my doctor was Dr. Webber Pals. She outlined
the plan. So, although I wanted surgery right away to get this
damn thing out of me quickly, they need to shrink the tumor first.
So I am scheduled to receive 3 rounds of chemo (each round is a
21day cycle. Hey sounds like my period. LOL! It used to be 28
days but it keeps getting shorter. I wonder if that is just a
coincidence – that the cycle sort of matches our cycle.) After the
chemo, surgery, then 3 more rounds of chemo after my hysterectomy.
(Damn the stomach was just starting to get flat again with all my
healthy eating!) I received a whole pile of information about the
specific type of chemo drugs I will be receiving and the potential
side effects. Yes I will go bald! That is apparently one of the
least of my worries as far as side effects go! They have this
down pat. The information tells me what reaction I will have on
which day!

Day 1: chemo treatment.

Day 1-3: nausea, therefore anti-nausea drugs. Perhaps constipation
they say. Stool softener and mover . . . who knew two separate
pills for that!??

Day 4-6: aching muscles like when you get the flu, extra strength
Tylenol. After that your white count drops – this is when you
are most susceptible to catching a cold, etc. This lasts for a
week.

By week three, your white count is building back up . . . just
to knock it down again. On top of that there are myriad of other
reactions that you can have including, neuropathy (tingling fingers
and toes), dry mouth, lack of appetite, de-hydration, hearing
problems, fingernails breaking and weakening. I never really thought
about it but the way chemo works is that it really doesn't attack
cancer cells per se . . . it attacks all rapidly multiplying
cells in your body ergo, hair loss, nails weakening etc. Anyway

the list of possible reactions is as long as anything a person hypersensitive about their condition can think of!

Carole

October 12, 2007
Subject Line: No Flu for you!

Hi Guys,

I have decided to combine all my mails into one mail with one massive email list! I would like to thank all of you who have sent me your best wishes and support. Many of my friends and Mitel co-workers have offered bids of support. It occurred to me that there is something tangible that people can do, that helps show support and benefits many others besides me.

I begin my chemotherapy this week and it was suggested that Josh, Dan and I get our flu shots. (Actually, I have no choice.) It occurred to me at that moment that as I go through this fight — the flu is the last thing I need. Even more importantly it occurred to me that I am a people person. I hate being alone. I hate missing out! I would love to stop in for a visit, but if my friends come in contact with the flu and I get it — it would be an added complication.

I have never received the flu shot in the past . . . always thinking that "well I never get the flu anyway" . . . but somehow missing the importance that quelling the flu may have on others around. Others whom may not even look sick but are vulnerable just the same." Shame on me." Well here is a chance for me to make amends for being remiss in this responsibility in the past.

I know that Brenda in the health unit at Mitel offers flu shots. I also know that the first flu shot clinic in Ottawa is going to be on Sat. October 27th at Holy Trinity School (in Kanata off Castlefrank) between 8:30 and 3:30.

Cheryl, friend of mine who is a nurse told me that even in our hospitals the average rate of the staff getting the flu shot is only 52%. She also says that the Public Health Unit Goal is 70% this year. Let's see if we can get 70% of Mitel and my friends getting their flu shot. I would love to come and visit everyone!

Carole

October 13, 2007
Subject: Keep an eye out for a little French lady

Hi Guys,

Noella (my mother in law) is down to help out. So, if you see a strange (you know what I mean), little French lady wandering around the village. Say hello! The house will never be cleaner!

Carole

October 15, 2007
Subject: Summoning the Heavens!

Hi Guys,

I just thought I would let you know that I got in a little earlier than expected. They called today and said 7:30 on Friday but then said they have an opening at 10:30 tomorrow – then they called and asked me to come in at 8:30. So I get my first Chemo treatment tomorrow at 8:30. I will keep you up to date and figure I need a few days to recover ;-) so for coffee club members, I will not be at coffee for a few days!

So really they are shoving poison into me . . . Let's hope it works well! I don't know . . . did all those late nights at darts work for training in my favor? That mix of Rye and Tequila must have helped me learn to function with all that crap in me ;-) (Okay I know some of you have helped clean up the puke . . . but really . . . how often did that happen – all things considered!) So far my "Hi Guys" list has people from all the major religions and a few not so main stream;-) So let's align all our chakras, get the Gods working in unison and send out all that Wiccan power of the summer solstice out into the universe at once . . . or whatever spiritual ritual works for you!

Thanks everyone – I know you are thinking about me!

Carole

October 16, 2007
Subject: First in 23 years . . .

Hi Guys,

I guess I should officially confirm. We are not hosting our annual Halloween Party. Somehow costumes, drinking and dancing until 4am to the Time Warp . . . just don't seem to be in the cards this year. Gee, even when I gave birth Oct 6 to Josh with a C-Section I was up partying for Halloween!

Next year!

Carole

October 16, 2007
Subject: They don't look sick . . .

Hi Guys,

First of all . . . Thank God for my Blackberry . . . coming to you live . . .

As I sit here, day one of chemo – there are seven of us. Three are older, probably in their late 50's or early 60's. Like me none of them look sick. I wonder if I have ever been less than nice to a lady, such as the ones in this room. Lesson: just because someone looks healthy, doesn't mean they are – must be doubly vigilant in my commitment to deliver random acts of kindness on a daily basis. The first I meet is Christine, she is only twenty – five and if she weren't in this clinic I would have thought she was a cute young lady in a quirky hat with extremely short hair. She is scheduled for surgery in a few weeks. Her mother is taking her

back to her apartment. The one Christine rented. She had moved from Windsor and found out she has ovarian cancer on the first day she was to start her Masters degree in at Carleton University. She seems upbeat, but unlike me I am sure she is mourning the loss of future children. Something I am all too familiar with. I feel fortunate that this is happening after having my son. I know this is something that will touch her life over and over again, long after the cancer has subsided and this treatment is no more than a memory. Another young woman is happy they have changed her chemo and medications because her acne has subsided??? She is another woman at an early point in her life – I imagine that finding her soul mate looms largely on her mind. Two of the older ladies are by themselves and I wonder what their situation is. One is very concerned about myriad symptoms. I think she is alone and afraid. Another is quiet and simply relaxing. The final lady is with her husband. She is on other, "non cancer" related medications. They ask her lots of questions. As for me I am healthy, short of allergy shots (which apparently are not contra-indicated) are all the medication I am on. As I look around the room. I feel blessed, young enough that I am healthy, old enough that I already have a wonderful husband and child. There are many instructions to read and remember, but I have Dan. There are social workers telling us to keep an eye on our son. I take heed but am already comforted in knowing that when Hillary Clinton wrote "it takes a village to raise a child" I literally have a village happy to help raise my child in this time of battle.
Carole

October 16, 2007
Subject: Tequila on tap!

Hi Guys,

I am in the middle of mt treatment – gotta love Blackberries! So my hunch was right! When I got here, my pharmacist or "poison pusher" as I like to call her asked me a few questions. The question of interest was "do you have issues with alcohol?" Thinking she was concerned about whether or not I was an alcoholic, I quickly responded that occasionally I drink a few too many red wines on a Saturday night but that honestly my drinking was limited. She then told me that they were worried if I had a tolerance issue since the Taxol, is delivered in alcohol. Well now I laugh! "No my tolerance for alcohol is quite high" – thanks to all the Rye and Tequila training! LOL. See I knew all those long, late nights at darts was good training!

The "poison pusher" a beautiful woman in her 30's is actually working on a study to see if they can speed up the I.V. time – but they are worried about a patient receiving the equivalent of 2 whole drinks in one hour! LOL again – come to Fitzroy Harbour we are trained to tolerate twice that!!

Got to pee again – talk to all of you soon . . . In the immortal words of Earnest Ainsley "evil spirits come out!!)

See you soon,

Carole

October 18, 2007
Subject: I feel good dada dada da da da . . .

Hi Guys,

Well it is day 2 after my first chemo session. In a nutshell, I feel good. The anti – nausea drugs seem to be working – or perhaps again it was all the practice drinking way to much rye and tequila not only prepared me for the chemo itself (for those whom I just added to this mailing list . . . they deliver the chemo in alcohol and the nurse was concerned about my ability to handle the equivalent of two drinks in one hour LOL) but apparently it has also helped my ability to overcome nausea! Okay perhaps the progress with anti – nausea drugs has helped too ;-)

Anyway I feel fine. I do want to tell you that before my chemo they had a plethora of people come talk to me about the treatment. A social worker came by to see how I was managing. Her first question was "Do you have a support network?" Again I laugh . . . with all of you supporting me, in so many wonderful ways! Dan and I quickly convinced her we were covered on that front and she actually said, "I'd like to move to Fitzroy Harbour – it sounds wonderful." Truly it is. All of you in Fitzroy and other places are helping me feel confident that this is just a small hurdle.

In case I hadn't mentioned this earlier – yes I will be bald soon. I have decided to get a hair cut first – as a transition and yes, yes, I know . . . my hair has been the same since high school – so now is my chance to be adventuresome with my hair. If it sucks it'll be gone in a few weeks anyway! If I like it I may keep it short after all this is done. I promise I will take a digital picture and email it to everyone next week.

In case anyone is interested, it was interesting to see the other ladies receiving treatment the day I was in. I feel very lucky. I think if you have to have this happen to you I am at the perfect age. I am done having kids, yet young enough that I really am quite healthy . . . and oh by the way according to the View this morning (my new morning pastime) today is International Menopause day – who knew. Anyway, just when things were starting to be a pain down there, (no graphic detail - you're welcome Patrick!) I am going to be done with it.

I don't have a date for surgery yet, but according to my guess at timing it will be near Christmas. The rub of all this, is the day I found out I had ovarian cancer I got my period. BAM! Kick you where it hurts . . . not only that - I guess I have another period or two to deal with before it's done. Seems kinda like throwing good money after bad. LOL . . . such is the life of a woman.

Okay - now another thing on my mind. Some of you don't know but at the wise old age of 35 I got a tattoo. And of course, with me, logic always prevails . . . even when I'm trying to be wild . . . . I got it so that even in a bikini I could hide it. Very low down on my front hipbone! Again, me being not so girlie and not wanting a flower or butterfly or anything like that I got the Chinese character for "play". (Directions for Dan I guess???!!!) Well now I am worried that when they do the surgery it's going to come out looking like a Rorschach ink block test or the Chinese character for "I told you, you'd regret it"!

Oh well enough for today. Thanks again to all of you. You provide me strength, joy and laughter!

Carole

October 19, 2007
Subject: Haircut ideas!

Hi Guys,

OKAY so she's beautiful. But imagine a slightly older, a slightly fatter faced, slightly larger nosed lady and voila you have me :-) Her hair looks messy . . . perfect. I don't need to spend time working on it. Anyone wishing to offer suggestions of slightly more adventuresome, ideas send a photo!

Carole

October 20, 2007
Subject: Forget about it . . .

Hi Guys,

Well I was supposed to feel "achy' for the last 3 days, nothing.
Okay it felt a little aching after watching an 8-hour Marathon
viewing of the last season of the Soprano's with Brian. I did
not need any of the "optional" drugs for nausea, constipation or
even the extra strength Tylenol for aches and pains . . . this
seems simple so far . . . and hair's in tact!

My medicine chest is starting to look like a pharmacy. Thank
goodness for a good drug plan and there's an Access card you can
apply for and you can get all these drugs for $1.00. Hope you
never need it but its there!

Carole

October 23, 2007
Subject: We are experiencing technical
            difficulties . . .

Hi Guys,

I am half way to having my email on my PC up and running. (This is
on my Blackberry.) So I'm thinking, as everyone waits with bated
breath to see my new haircut – I realize that not only do I have
short hair, something my head has not seen since grade 10, but I
am now writing daily, (thanks Ivan :-) a passion since grade 6, I
have to ask myself if I am heading in the right direction? What's
next? Peeing issues? Wait – stop laughing – ya okay, I already
have those! Another digression . . . So this is what this journey
is about . . . Several steps back for a giant leap forward. I am
even confusing myself . . . must be the drugs??

I keep reminding myself that I am sick – not bad I think! When
someone says it's surreal . . . being told you have cancer IS
the epitome of surreal! I keep forgetting I am sick. Thanks to
all of you. I am truly blessed to have such wonderful friends.
Thanks for lending me your email ear. These emails are such an

important part of my day! (This from the friend who used to respond to your emails explaining, "even if I don't have time to respond to your email, fill out the email quiz or whatever, I am reading them.") Now I am in jeopardy of causing you dismissal from your jobs – due to distraction from your duties with my onslaught of emails! Anyway my mother in law heard expletives fly yesterday after calls to Bell and two to my router vendor. I didn't swear to the guys on the phone but Dan heard my frustration when I called him and my mother in law downstairs heard too. Ahhh she's used to the occasional slip up in my otherwise demure behavior LOL! It solidified how much these emails mean and I was so mad that I pissed the day away trying to fix something that I needed so much! Shows how much technology has changed our lives!

One more thing, Agathe, a friend in Fitzroy, showed me her quilting today. She heads up the guild in Ottawa that makes quilts for cancer patients. Someone has requested one for me, so apparently I will be getting one soon. If anyone has cotton fabric that they don't want they can donate it to Victoria quilts for future quilts for cancer patients. They do amazing things even with small pieces. Let me know if you have any that you would like to donate and I will find out the best way to get it to the quilters. I personally have a fabric fetish and have fabric that has been sitting in bins for years waiting for something. So let me know if you have any to donate.

Talk to you soon,

Carole

October 23, 2007
Subject: Hair cut

Hi Guys,

Here's a picture of my hair! I figure no matter what it looks like I'm good – who would have the balls to tell a woman with ovarian cancer her hair sucks ;-)

Carole

October 23, 2007
Subject: Re: Hair cut

Hi Carole, Dan, Josh and Noella,

It was so great hearing from you Carole. You have a great attitude, as this is so important. You just have to remember "Bald is beautiful as the McCaskill men have always said.

When you were all down here Mae and I said that you were a very strong lady and Dan and Josh were lucky to have you, so keep up the faith. Just remember all our prayers are always with you at all times. We love you all.

Kirk and his family had to evacuate their home at 5:30 am 2 days ago and took very little except the clothes on their backs. Kirk said they were told at the time that there was a 90% change they would lose their home. We have had no further word as of yet. I will try to get hold of Kirk today.

Love
Ted & Mae

October 23, 2007
Subject: Re: Hair cut

Ted,

Thanks so much for your thoughts and prayers. Our thoughts will be with Kirk and his family. Such an upheaval has to be tough on the kids especially. Send them our love and remind them that they will be able to replace the material things and a fire can never take their memories!

Love,
Carole, Dan, Josh and Noella!

October 30, 2007
Subject: Spidey Senses

Hi Guys,

I haven't emailed in a few days. I have been participating in some retail therapy. To Costco, with whom else but Patrick and to Winners, with my mother-in-law, then out again this morning! I just want to confirm in case you weren't sure . . . there is a connection between shopping and stress relief.

Over the last 3 days I have noticed a few things: 1/ hair in my hand when I run my hand through my hair and 2/ my scalp tingling and 3/my head feeling like I banged it. A week ago I felt pain directly on my ovaries . . . which I concluded was the chemo attacking "quickly duplicating cells" . . . since they hadn't mentioned that pain specifically. As for my scalp, nobody said anything to me about my scalp pain so I assumed that too was my acutely developed senses, highly evolved nerve endings, or of course, in my house, full of superhero paraphernalia, I had to consider the fact that I might just have "Spidey senses".

It was coming. I could feel it. Hair loss is just around the corner.

So this morning my illusions of super powers and delusions of grandeur were squashed in one fell swoop. This morning I went to the Wig Lady. Obviously much more in touch with the realities of hair loss she burst my bubble. I didn't even mention it to her when she starting telling me about the tingling. I hadn't discovered! I didn't have ultra tuned senses after all. In fact I just hadn't been told about these normal sensations. Ahhh, so much for the letter to the New England Journal of Medicine, or at least the Canadian Cancer Society!

She (the Wig Lady) asks what I want. I tell her "short – kinda like it is now only combed nicer . . . and perhaps with blonde highlights." One minute later she comes out with the wig that I will ultimately buy. Over $600 later, she has done her job, short of one thing. We have agreed on the wig – confirmed of course by Dan and Josh who were with me. (Josh had a doctor appointment – I didn't pull him out of school just to approve my wig – in case you were wondering ;-) I digress, back on track. Wig style confirmed, funny little caps chosen to keep my head warm at night and around the house. She says, a matter-of-factly, "I can shave your head now." WHOA!!!!!! SCREECH>>>>SLAM ON THE BREAKS. This was not part of my day's plan. "You can wear the wig home," she states – again almost sounding glib. She then explains how the weight of the hair pulls on the weakened roots and makes your scalp hurt. Okay nobody told me that either – I only got my hair cut short because it seems like a logical time to take the leap to something new after over 30 years of the same long hair style! Apparently Dan's length is not good either (a number 1 on the razor) – in case of a nick that could cause infection. Perhaps I should have just chosen a cut like Cathy or Ivan. Still I am not ready. I have determined that while I have no problem losing my hair, I do have two worries. One, my profile without hair will really enhance my nose . . . ergo the need for a wig, but two I realize that once I have no hair, strangers will know I have cancer and I am not ready for the "oh poor her – look she has cancer" look followed closely by the "Best Wishes smile".

. . . and I only spend about ahhh 5 minutes max on my hair – I can't imagine how tough this is for some women!

So I have learned two things today: 1/ Doctor's tell you about the side effects that make you not feel your best, . . . the Wig lady tells you about the side effects that make you not look your best . . . and 2/ There's nothing like 20 minutes of shopping to strengthening your resolve keeping your right brain busy while your left brain ratifies what must be done . . . in other words – shopping therapy works. Two new sweaters and a new winter coat later – all in a size smaller than last year . . . without even trying, I have decided to get my head "shaved" on Friday . . . pictures may or may not be forthcoming ;-)

So aside from a few emotional issues and revelations, I feel great!

Carole

PS. I stopped at the pharmacy to pick up false eyelashes . . . I can't see my self with no eyelashes. The clerk asks, "Oh are these for Halloween?" She kinda caught me off guard . . . so all I said was "No, cancer." I think I freaked her out. I smiled and said "its okay."

October 30, 2007
Subject: We're all connected

Hi Guys,

It is my intention for this cancer to be gone, completely gone.
I have avoided the Internet sites with the many sad stories that
accompany such a disease. However, every so often I inadvertently
stumble across something. I believe in the power of intention,
positive thinking or whatever you chose to call it. Deep in the
recesses of my mind however, I am acutely aware that I must live
each day to the fullest. I think I can do that for the next 30
years. I have too much to do, too many plans and time to spend
with Dan and much more to do for Josh.

I chose not to find out too much. I chose instead to do as my
doctors suggest while throwing in holistic, natural and logical
changes to my life. This is how I have felt about dieting. I have
never gone on a diet. I have changed my life style to adapt to
my changing body. I will do the same now. I will do those things
that intuitively feel right for me. Some things I see, I scoff
at, while others just make sense. I believe that I can make that
big a difference. Only time will tell.

I guess like everyone facing their own mortality, they find something
important they must do. For me, it is writing, but for me it also
supporting the planet. I think I have found that my spirituality is
based on "God", being inside each and everyone of us. And each and
every one of us is connected – not just to each other but also to
everything in nature. This is where I have received my strength, my
conviction and my comfort. I realize I am not afraid to die – I am
just afraid of leaving the ones I love. These two things are not the
same. The result though is that I know I must help myself but also I
must do what I can to help the environment. We can make a difference
and I will do what I can to help ensure people become aware of
what we are doing. We need to look at root cause analysis instead
of piecing together band-aid solutions that do not fix the problems
and only line the pockets of our hyper driven capitalistic society.

Carole

November 1, 2007

Hi Ken and Judy,

Thanks so much for having us over for Halloween dinner. It was a great time. It helped fill the void of us not hosting our Halloween party for the first time in 23 years! Next year we will be back at my house dancing in the living room in our costumes!

Carole

November 2, 2007
Subject: Only in Canada eh?

Hi Guys,

No I am not talking about tea (if you remember the tag line from the commercial . . .) I am sitting in the waiting room of the lab to get my blood work done (now that I have cancer my CA125 blood test is paid for by OHIP) prior to my next Chemo.
There are easily 18 people waiting. All ages, races and economic statuses! How do I know this you ask? Aside from the normal cues, there is one other man with his head buried in a Blackberry. Upon closer investigation – I recognize him, I smile at him, and he does not recognize me! Oh ya, the short hair, darker than it has ever been. The man is Terry Matthews. Make that Sir Terrence Matthews, founder of Mitel, Newbridge and a plethora other high tech companies. Yes, Terry was knighted by Queen Elizabeth. Yes, Terry is a billionaire – with his own private jet, with two pilots so they can trade off flying versus down time, for mandatory rest periods . . . in order to meet Terry's hectic schedule. Yes, Terry has a private enclave here in Kanata with several acres, all the normal amenities of wealth including pool, tennis court, and putting green and of course a 25-foot half pipe used in the past by his youngest son to skateboard on, in the privacy of his backyard. Let's not forget the guarded gatehouse. This is his life. It is not my intention by any means, to cast aspersions on his life style. He works hard for what he has. He has a plane because he travels so much and wants to get back home with his family instead of spending time in airports. He has gated property because, as anyone that wealthy, there is always the threat of kidnapping.

Armed with the knowledge of just how Terry lives, I can tell you why I love Canada so much! Universal Health Care! If you ever doubted it – now you can believe it! Terry was killing time on his Blackberry just like me. We all wait. Yes, we may complain about the waiting but it gives me great comfort knowing we ALL wait.

I know . . . Universal health care isn't "only in Canada, you say" but I know it is one more reason why I love living in Canada.

Carole.

P.S Tips you can use: go to labs after lunch especially on a Friday. The lady says it's always packed in the morning. Also, I bet lots of working people take longer lunches on Fridays at their local restaurants, which makes the labs less crowded.

November 2, 2007
Subject: Where's the road rage when you need it!

Hi Guys,

My new 'hair' now sits beside my treadmill. Perhaps a peek at the future usefulness of this item! I left the house this morning with a messy version of my new short, light brown hairdo, I returned with an ear length do, with blonde and strawberry blonde highlights with wispy bangs my second trip to the wig lady begins . . .

My real hair is very messy, not wanting to wash it over the last few days, knowing that with each rub, hundreds of hairs would find their way to the bathtub drain. (Not that the hair loss is the bother here, but the fact that cleaning hair out of the drain has been a trigger for my hyperactive gag reflex for years.) Even the simple action of putting my sunglasses on my head resulted in hair in my hands and trapped in the arm of my glasses.

As I drive down the 416 on my way back to the Wig Lady, I begin to laugh hysterically. No not about my hair as I am now prepared. My laughter is about my wish . . . I am wishing for someone to cut me off, show a lack of courtesy to me in some way or to generally piss me off. Why would I wish for this you ask? Because I don't want to miss a once in a lifetime opportunity! I can picture myself feigning a fit of rage, yelling loudly at some asshole's lack of courtesy and then LITERALLY pulling my hair out!!!! What have I got to lose – nothing that won't be gone today anyway? Imagine the look on the poor guy's face, as my hair came tumbling to the ground in clumps as my head began to resemble a patchwork quilt. Seriously – once in a lifetime . . . missed.

The Wig Lady cut my hair, washed it and then shaved it on 4. This left about a half inch of hair. Very smooth, very tingly. Nice . . .

Apparently leaving the hair this length will ensure a soft feel on the head when the wig is worn. If cut right down, the hair is hard and can hurt the scalp with the weight of the wig on it. She assures me it will continue to fall out – perhaps without so much "pain". She then puts on the wig, fluffs it up:
"Never wear a wig too flat – then it looks like a wig," I am informed.
"There are little cuts in the wig that go around the ears – use this to align the wig"
"There are little wires on the side near the temple – press these in so there the wig doesn't gape"

I thought wigs would be easy but apparently THERE is a skill to wigs. I have read *The Art of War*, but I even missed the Coles notes version of The Art of Wig Wearing. Despite all of this training, Dan suggests I try putting it on myself! I place the wig on my head, align it, flick some strands behind my ears, adjust the bangs and venture out of the store into the big wide world. First stressor – will my sunglasses fit over the wig? Under it? Do they push the hair back so you can see my own hair? A quick check in the mirror and everything still looks okay. Off for more shopping – apparently turtlenecks (half my winter wardrobe are hard with wigs because they sit so high on your neck – unless of course you are Iman or a Somali lady who has gone through that neck stretching ceremony where they keep adding metal chokers to their necks to lengthen them. I shop. At the checkout counter, a lady smiles . . . did I knock my wig or is she just being nice? Ah ha, she likes the Santa I have pulled out of my cart. Still, I wonder.

I get in the car and adjust the wig. It feels like it is riding up the back of my neck. Wait. Did I just rotate it? Better check in the mirror. It looks flat. I should "fluff or puff" it up. Shit, now it just looks messy. Try again. Too flat! Okay. Relax. Re-adjust, align it, check the part, and fluff it up. Now I am driving, and peeking at myself in the rearview mirror. At a stoplight, I grab the wig and hoist it down lower on my forehead. Okay, the man in the van next to me – just saw that. Of course he's staring now. I will need to remember that one! I need a bathroom with a locking door and a mirror bigger than the 2-inch wide rearview mirror I have been using. I finally see myself. Done! It's not as bad as I imagined. Ahhh, stress gone! On to another store!

There is one thing that is certain. Despite this new skill set I need to develop, nobody will believe it is my hair. It is way more coiffed than my hair has ever been!

Carole

November 2, 2007
Subject: Points for and Against

Hi Guys,

As a Tomboy and avid sports fanatic, I feel I must have a sport's Pros and Cons cancer thing going.
Let's count it out:

Pros

It seems to have opened every creative vein in my body!

It has connected me with many whom I never really new cared as much as they do.

It has connected old friends. Not just mine, but people I know, who know each other, but hadn't been in contact with each other until they saw a name on my email list.

It has made me realize I look good with short hair.

It has made me lose weight – I know – but it had to be said.

It has made me cherish each and every day.

It has changed my perspective on what is important and what I need to be happy.

It has made my already good eating habits in to ridiculously good eating habits.

It has made me tell my sister and brother I love them. Something I hadn't said in a while.

It has made my husband and I even closer after 27 years together.

It has made me realize that being pleasant in circumstances where others choose chaos is the only way to go.

It has made me realize how helpful people are and how if they are not – they probably have a good reason.

It has made me realize that people who don't look sick often are – so be nice to everyone.

It made me realize that I have lots left to do and so I can't possibly die.

It made me realize how very positive I have been all my life and especially now.

It has made me realize that I am spiritual and that I believe God is within each of us and that we are one with nature and have a duty to rebalance the power on this earth.

It made me realize that I like my role as the logical strong friend with all the good remedies for what is bothering us . . . even it is me that is in the crisis. Conversely it has made me realize that I too need help.

It has made me realize that money can't buy health but that even in Canada where we have universal health care, having a good job, with a great benefits plan, really adds to peace of mind and helps in the healing process.

It re-affirms that taking back an ounce of control through knowledge is a solid foundation in recovery.

It allows me to emulate one of my favorite stars Rene Russo in the movie *Thomas Crown Affair* by drinking a disgusting looking but healthy green concoction.

Cons

I have cancer and the implications that could go along with it.

Carole

November 5, 2007
Subject: Re: Where's the road rage when you need it!

Good Morning all! Hope your week is fab! Just a note I had dinner with Carole Saturday night . . . and must say she looks great! She walked into the room looking hip & very stylish and walked out with a completely different look but remained hip and stylish! Awesome!

Annette

November 05, 2007
To: Annette
Subject: RE: Where's the road rage when you need it!

Hi I'm Viv, Carole's cousin from England. It was great to read your e mail re dinner with Carole I'm glad she's having fun. When she was over with us a couple of years ago I laughed more in 10 days than I had in 10 months she's hilarious. It's great for me to be able to keep in touch with her by email.

Viv

November 5, 2007
Subject Re: Where's the road rage when you need it!

Hello Viv, Carole's cousin from England! We do a quarterly dinner together with two other couples and it was scheduled for next weekend. Carole will be going through another bought of chemo and we decided to move it up a week. As you know from her emails, her spirits are great and we all love laughing with her!

Annette

November 6, 2007
Subject: Note to self

Hi Guys

It's my first time out in public without hair and no wig. We stop at
Tim Horton's on our way for my second chemo session. I feel much
better because my hair is not askew, so when I walked into the
bathroom imagine my chagrin when I realized that the combined look
of my bald head and super big dark sunglasses makes me look like a
frickin' FLY! Note to self, buy new sunglasses on my way home.

I asked if they would mix my chemo with a good red wine this time as
I find it is a nicer buzz than clear liquors. They did not comply.

All is going well today. Listening and watching Van the Man on a
DVD on my laptop as I rack up a 6-hour bar bill . . . and typing
away on my Blackberry!

Later,

Carole

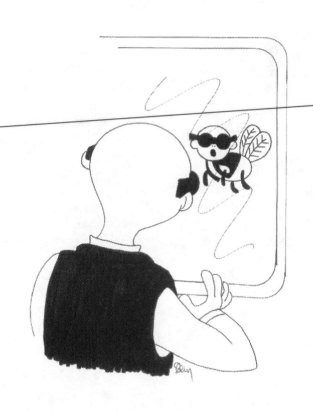

November 6, 2007
Subject: Round 2 – Ding!

Hi Guys,

Okay so I am not Superman. Even though sometimes I think I am! That's the influence of Dan and Josh and my house full of tiny little statues called Hero Clix, (mini statues of comic book super heroes) our dedication to watching Heroes and 6 foot murals of super heroes donning the walls of my house. With this atmosphere it is no wonder I came into my chemo session this morning with the dream of a 10 year old boy, that somehow my regenerative super hero abilities may have kicked in and the nurses would tell me the cancer was all gone. Apparently I do not have super hero powers but I did have very good reaction to the chemo. As I progress through the stages of the chemo treatment, I again have a very positive experience. I have not felt any nausea, and aside from an occasional tingling in my finger, a slight headache and mild pain in my ovaries (the chemo blasting the cancer ala space invaders) I have felt great through all of this. My friend actually said this morning that I am "actually blossoming with Chemo!" This is somewhat true. I looked back at a picture from early Sept. I seem bloated in the face. I have bags under my eyes and just don't look good at all. Even without hair I look much better than I did before I was being treated. As Dan said the other day, he used to think of the bald head of cancer as bad, but it's actually a good thing because the loss of hair simply means that the chemo is attacking quickly duplicating cells – which along with cancer cells include our hair cells – so a day without my hair is a day that the chemo is beating up the cancer! I foresee a TKO in round 6!

Carole

November 6, 2007
Subject: Savasana

Hi Guys,

I went to yoga last night. First of all, although I am new to this, let me tell you, yoga is way easier than 3 weeks ago when I was trying to do the cobra (lay flat on stomach arms bent at side and lift head and chest off the ground) with 10 pounds of fluid in my belly! Yoga, no pain, lots of stretching, deep breathing and only a mild form of hair loss . . . Yes that's right! Like most, I have one of those yoga mats made to grip your feet so you don't slip. As I lay back in Savasana, a position where you are laying flat on your back, I felt the grip, on my very loose and frail hair. Next thing I know the back of my head has adopted the look of "The Thousand Islands," a spattering of hair dotted amongst a sea of skin. I quickly don my ball cap and resume my deep, therapeutic breathing. I will come again to yoga as much as I can. Breathe . . .

Carole

November 8, 2007
Subject: Hosting the Coffee Club!

Hi Cathy and Leo,

I wanted to send you a mail of Thanks. As you know I have been a "member" of the coffee club since well before Tom and Ursula, back to Marc and Sue. It has always been a wonderful part of my love of Fitzroy Harbour. The Harbour Store coffee club has provided a wonderful meeting place for Harbourites and visitors alike. It is a place to meet and discuss, just about anything under the sun. It has brought together a unique group of people over the years, all from varying ages, backgrounds and interests. Looking at all who frequent the coffee club, one would wonder what brings us all together and how we can all be connected. I have even planned my work hours to accommodate this rich opportunity for sharing ideas, opinions and mostly sharing laughs. Now that I am somewhat homebound, I have a whole new appreciation for the value of the coffee club! I now join the ranks of some of its members who have found their daily dose of human interaction at the coffee club.

I send these thanks, out to you. All of us that attend the coffee club on a regular basis truly appreciate you letting us hang out in your back room on the cold and wet days and filling your picnic table on the warm and sunny days.

As always, see you tomorrow morning,

Carole

November 8, 2007
Subject: Cuffs and Collar . . .

Hi Guys,

If you are at all shy about your anatomy don't read this. This is where I will tell you all the things that you won't read anywhere else.

I am sure everyone is curious so I'll go ahead and tell you. Apparently you are supposed to lose your pubic hair as well. Come on, its hair just like the stuff on your head. However here is

the caveat . . . at least according to Carole. It will probably
be the last to go. So far, this is proving to be true. How do
I know this you ask? About 10 years ago . . . around the same
time I thought getting a tattoo on my hip was a good idea, I
also thought it would be a good idea to rid my self of my bikini
line hair for ever. So Sonya and I set out on our quest. As our
treatments began I realized that although Sonya had been the
wimpier of the two of us at the tattoo parlor, she was fairing
much better than me at electrolysis. Without a flinch, as the
high-speed ink needle plunged my skin and my giggles at Sonya's
obviously lower pain threshold, I now wished I had not been so
cavalier about my friend's discomfort. As the single electrically
charged needle targeted stray hairs along my panty line, my leg
flinched uncontrollably. It was now her turn to giggle.

After our second 20-minute session with no visible results, I made
the decision that it would be my last. Hers had fallen out and
stayed out. Mine had hung on, leaving me no alternative but to wax,
shave or forgo my bathing suit. This is how I know that my pubic
hair is going to hang on to the very last minute. As anyone knows
who has ventured down there with tweezers – they are strong roots!

D'oh! It seems obvious when I think about it but . . . they
didn't tell me this. I have been bleeding like a stuck pig for a
month. Yes a month. The day I went to emergency. The day of my
diagnosis of ovarian cancer was the day I got my period, right
in the hospital as I was awaiting a trans-vaginal ultrasound.
Hum, as a tampon person this does present a dilemma . . . in or
out? Obviously out . . . apologies required but such is life. I
digress. So after my normal weeklong period, I get in for my first
chemo treatment and two days later I start to bleed again. Not too
much, yet is this normal? I search my Chemo side effects guide.
Nothing! Certainly bleeding would have been mentioned somewhere.
Then the piercing pain starts. I can feel little stabs directly
on my ovaries. This pain is constant. Still it is better than the
bloating from my ten-pound alien baby I had been carrying around
with me earlier in the month. I presume the pain is the chemo working
so I am not at all bothered by it. However the bleeding . . . I am
now wearing the biggest "super-duper-you-must-be anemic tampon,"
coupled with an "I'm one step down from a Depends" maxi pad and
switching them out every hour! Certainly this warrants a call to
the cancer clinic nurses? My first call to the cancer clinic! The

message says if it is an emergency dial 1, if not leave a message and we will get back to you in three days. Decision time . . . I decide although this is not technically an emergency, I would opt for emergency, worrying that if I waited for 3 days I might bleed out! A phone call later after re-assuring them that I actually feel fine, aside from the blood letting, I am told this is normal due to the assault on my ovaries. D'oh! I knew that. I hate when I miss things like that. Anyway another thing they don't tell you! It did slow down but I am still bleeding. Again another coincidence – there had been a special on tampons and with extra Air Miles points, I had bought enough for three months, but now I was below my "Be Prepared" threshold. For the first time in my marriage Dan needs to buy me more. Again this is not that big an issue, as I realize I will only have my period for a month or two more, then my reproductive system goes into forced retirement, instead of what I thought I was going to be the more, modern route with the "progressive retirement" approach to menopause;-)

By the way another tip you can use. Club Soda is the best stain remover.

Sarah thanks for the new/British terminology used in the Subject line in this mail!

Carole

November 8, 2007
Subject: BHI

Hi MJ, Judy, Connie and Carol,

Perhaps it is time to rename our Investment Club. I know that 10 years ago Big Hair Investments was a great name (Thanks Ted!) but I think it is now time to change it to Bald Head Investments – what do ya think? Now it's just a thought . . . . and I know we need to vote on it, but we wouldn't even have to change our bank account name. BHI still works!

. . . Doug – thanks for reminded me about our name the other day at the store!

Carole

November 8, 2007
Re: Surgery date.

Hi Guys,

I have my surgery date. I go in Dec 21st. What a great Christmas present. Truly! The sooner they get this out of me the better. If I hadn't got in just before Christmas, I would have had to wait until Mid January. I am only in for 2 or 3 days so I should be home for Christmas. Perhaps a little drugged up but what's the difference? A little wine or morphine! Actually I'm pushing for something else since I puked my guts out when I was on morphine for my C - section.

I have to say that losing my hair was one thing - but with my pending hysterectomy, the thought of gaining a goatee is another thing - that's where I draw the line. Bald and a goatee . . . yes I will look like Dan ;-)

Carole

November 9, 2007
Subject: I knew I had an affinity with Winners.

Hi Guys,

As you guys know, I have become a staunch believer in retail therapy lately . . . okay, perhaps I always was. I just wanted to tell you that my favorite store . . . brand names at low prices . . . I know I sound like an ad but isn't it a coincidence that my favorite store Winners sponsors the Ovarian Cancer Walk for Hope. It is held *Labour* Day weekend . . . is there a joke there? Next year I will be walking and I invite any of you who want to, to join me! I'm sure we can raise a little money while having a blast like we normally do! A little walking, a little wine, a few snacks!

Carole

November 11, 2007
Subject: There's a joke in there somewhere

Hi Guys,

"So the gay man, the bald cancer patient and the working mother
of 5 walk into a Chapters . . ." I know there is a joke there
somewhere, as I start to giggle on my latest "therapeutic sojourn
into the heart blood of our capitalistic society!"

Thank God I am no longer driving into Ottawa to work everyday,
I am sure my retail therapy is managing to come in, less than
my old weekly gas expense to and from work. Seriously doesn't
our little trio sound like the opening to a not so Politically
Correct joke?

Keeping on the theme of feeding capitalism . . .

Books on Cancer – diet & lifestyle changes	$80.00
A wireless card for my Laptop	$45.00
Cute little black boots that lace-up with Pompom's	$59.00
A day out of the house shopping with friends:	Priceless

Carole

November 13, 2007
Subject: Get down tonight . . . .

Hi Guys,

I went to see my oncologist today. Although the disco beat and
sounds of "Do a little dance. Make a little love. Get down
tonight . . ." plays over and over again in my head, *Dr. Fung Ke
Fung and the Chemo Crew* band fail to appear. It is Dan's and my
goal to see this man at least once. I am sure we will break into
"the hustle" or a disco arm roll with the "white man's overbite"
when we see him.

Nor do I see Dr. Le my official oncologist (by the way the man
that I've only seen once for 1/2 hour and who has inflicted more
pain to me with two digits, then anyone should have to endure!)
Instead I get a wonderful young woman, Dr. Webber-Pals, whom has
lots of good news for me. First my C125 blood test results went
from my baseline of 3335 to 935 in just one chemo session!! This
is great – however a normal level is just 35! No I did not miss
a digit (different digit then the one mentioned above he-he!)

Anyway, the fluid has not returned. Another good sign! And I have
not had any adverse reactions so far. They tell me I am responding
very well to the chemo!!!!

So I have been asked to participate in a new chemo "delivery" system.
The drugs are the same but instead of injecting it intravenously;
they install a catheter, surgically installed under my skin near
my ribs that provide a conduit directly into my abdomen.
They will inject the chemo into the catheter – into my abdomen.
They have already had great success with this method as the chemo
gets directly to the affected area. So my last 3 or 4 treatments
after the surgery will be done this way.

I have also signed over my tumor to the "tumor bank". That's one
deposit I don't want back and hope to only make one deposit. Go
Research!
I believe I already made a deposit to the egg bank for research – I
wonder if it would help to put the two together kind of a before
and after type picture . . . seriously though I wonder if they
could learn something . . . ??

Again I feel lucky, as this new delivery method has already been proven more effective and it is not be offered at all cancer centers and not to everyone. Keep the good vibes coming girls!!! And remember . . . do a little dance, make a little love, get down tonight, with Fung Ke Fung!

Thanks everyone for your moral and spiritual support!

Carole

November 14, 2007
Subject: beating the odds

Hi Guys,

Despite having absolutely positive news yesterday about my CA125 count and being asked to participate in the new chemo delivery trial. I have been sad. This new trial has proven so far, on average, to add 16 months to a patient's life. I want 16 years. I want even more. I have geared my self up to overcome this. Perhaps I am foolish. I have so much I want to do. I have so much life left in me. I have always been a strong powerful woman. And yet I start to second guess my resolve. I slept awful last night. I feel less hungry today. I feel just a little bit more pins and needles than normal. It is easy to see how steep a slope I am hovering on. I am sure it is normal to have a bad day. I am sure the barrage of chemicals aimed at my ovaries is playing havoc with my hormones. Perhaps this sad mood is a new version of PMS.

I try not to dwell on any negative feelings whatsoever and for 6 weeks now I have been very successful. This time the feeling lingers. I have not sent this mail out because I do not want sympathy, only companionship. I don't want pity, only support. I do not want miracles, only to overcome what I know my mind and body is capable of achieving.

As is typical of me, when I have an emotion I do not want to feel, I examine why I am feeling this way. It may seem easy given my condition. However, I assure you it is not a simple matter of "I feel sorry for myself and for those things that I may lose out on. There is usually and underlying fear, worry or concern that is at the root cause of the emotion. This analysis has always provided me with the insight to move beyond. Like all people who are positive in their lives, I find a way to resolve these feelings. When I think about how I feel. I am most concerned with my family and how they will fare if I lose this battle. What conversations do I need to have, when do I have them. How do I smooth the way for those I love. I realize I have time. I realize that I just need to double my resolve. Focus on the things that are important. For me, for my family and for my friends!

Today I resolve:

- To enjoy every moment
- To do everything for me that I need to do and to believe it deep inside
- To focus on my family – to create lasting and loving memories
- To keep writing, for me, for others – that they may benefit
- To support nature – to acknowledge the connection we have with nature and to act as her proxy in the human world
- To spread joy and happiness to everyone I can – not just because it is just a good thing to do, but also because, I believe in Karma
- To understand and appreciate what is truly important and what isn't

Today I acknowledge that although my life is clearly divided into "Before" and "After" I acknowledge that everyone faces an after and that none of us knows where and when it will happen. My before is only different because it has a clear line of delineation . . . for some of us we wait for the after and for me I have the strength and the resolve to help shape my after.

Carole

November 15, 2007
Subject: this program delayed until . . .

Hi Guys,

I just found out the city is trying to close down the Fitzroy Harbour community center. I will be spending the next few days reviewing the city budget and preparing a business case to support keeping it open.

For those of you in the Harbour you know how important the community center is to us, for those whom I work with, you know I will be formulating a viable, business case focused argument that will justify the expenditure.

I feel very energized! Nothing like a cause that you are passionate about to change your focus from yourself to something that will

help everyone . . . I thrive on this type of challenge . . . Oh
cancer you stand no chance now!!!!! I never knew how much I missed
Microsoft Powerpoint LOL!

Speak to all of you very soon!

Carole

November 15, 2007
Subject: Re: this program delayed until . . .

Hey,

Blessed are those who are fortunate to have a friend like
Carole!

Go get them Carole! I daresay the entire city doesn't stand a chance
now, and I'm confident we won't lose our community centre!

Sonya

November 15, 2007
Subject: Re: Re: this program delayed until . . .

Never mind Sonya . . . you should have seen her eyes bug out when
she talked about it this morning. I was so scared . . . I peed
a little.

Patrick

November 21, 2007
Subject: Volunteering

Hi Guys,

I just wanted to let you know I feel great. My hair is pretty much
all gone. I now feel like the many Fitzroy men who also need to
wear hats to cover their balding heads! There seems to be a very
large contingent of bald men in Fitzroy . . .

I have been working hard on reviewing the City of Ottawa budget – looking for stupidity . . . sadly I have found many instances . . . luckily this will help in our fight for the community center. Since I have been working on this fight with the city, my own fight has taken a turn . . . for the better. I have gotten off my lazy boy, I have been cooking (very healthy of course), cleaning and feeling much more like I am just a regular stay at home mom. I like this. I think it is a good feeling. I have volunteered my whole life, whether it was through Girl Guides, with the social committee at work, or with the community association. I think I have pulled back a little too far in this respect over the last few years. I am glad to be back involved with something for others that I feel passionate about. If you feel something is missing in your life – you might want to try it ;-)

Love you all!

Carole

November 21, 2007
Subject: 28 years

Hi Guys,

My email was not working yesterday . . . okay I messed up. I turned off my wireless connection D'oh! Anyway, I wanted to shout out to all of you that yesterday Dan and I celebrated 28 years "together", not married but when we officially started going out. I remember sitting in Dan's basement, he asked me to go out with him and I said "yes", and then added "its too bad how people go out and then ultimately hurt each other by breaking up" . . . I guess I was wrong! I cannot imagine how anyone can go through something like this without someone as loving and supportive as Dan. I know many of you are facing your own challenges and I hope you are as lucky as me. For those of you on the other side of the fence please know that your support and understanding is very much appreciated even if sometimes we forget to say it!

Carole

November 21, 2007
Subject: Re: 28 years

Carole,

God, are you trying to make me cry today? Its good, no worries . . . both emails were very good and words that someone "caught up in the craziness of day to day life" really, really needed to hear. Funny how your words are helping me in my life, supposed to be the other way around. Must be the Christmas emotions setting in.
I am sooooo glad to hear that everything is going better than planned. I think of you often and although I am not really a part of your "clan so to speak" I love hearing the updates and your sense of grounding in this obstacle that life has brought you.

Heather

November 21, 2007
Subject: Re: 28 years

Hi Heather,

Don't cry, but I am happy my words are touching you. I really believe that what I put out to the world I will get back (Karma, I guess ala "My Name is Earl!")

Cancer . . . what a wake up call to clarifying what is important in life!

See you at Christmas, if I don't see you sooner!

Carole

November 22, 2007
Subject: a mail I couldn't send . . .

Hi Josh,

You keep asking me what I want for Christmas. How can I tell you what's on my list?
This year I ask for 3 simple things:

My health,
Time
Yours and Dad's health and happiness

Nothing else matters.

I Love you,

Mom

November 25, 2007
Subject: Westport trip

Hi Peggy,

Thanks again for organizing our girls shopping trip to Westport.
Thanks to the rest of the gang for another "pee in your pants"
funny good time. What a wonderful way to get into the spirit of
Christmas.

Sally, Thanks so much for suggesting I buy the fur lined, "hunting
style, ear flaps" hat. With a baldhead I know this will keep me
warm.

Carole

November 28, 2007
Re: Chips . . . yummmmm

Hi Guys,

Just a quick update. I went in for round 3 of Chemo yesterday.
After a busy weekend with Dan's office Christmas party, shopping
in Westport, a football banquet and helping out at Josh's school,
I took the 6 hours of chemo to sleep.

I did notice the other women around me though . . . several of
them were eating Cheezies and Doritos . . . me I was drinking my
"green" drink. My green drink is a concoction of spinach, kiwi,
chlorophyll, wheat grass, sheep sorrel - burdock supreme, black
walnut, whey powder, gogi juice, noni juice, banana, cocoa, quark,
yogurt and cinnamon. All things that are supposed to be extremely
healthy for people going through chemo . . . so I wonder, am I
wasting my energy on this drink or am I helping myself . . .
while they chow down on ummmmm delicious trans fat fried potato
and chemical stuff???

I think I'll stick with my green drink . . . I really think they
should suggest to people that they eat healthier when they are
trying to get their bodies to focus its immune system and all its
power to heal and getting rid of the cancer . . . oh well maybe
its just me ;-)

Carole

November 28, 2007
Subject: No more drugs . . .

Hi Guys,

After two rounds of chemo and the automatic prescription for a plethora of "just in case drugs" I told them not to bother writing me a script for any more. I have yet to need any of these drugs. I really think my "cancer diet," loads of hydration all have helped stave off most of the side effects. I am really starting to believe how true the idiom is "you are what you eat" and "your body is a temple." We eat way too many bad things . . . including chemicals.

Carole

November 30, 2007
Subject: Winter Solstice

Hi Guys,

Dec 21st – winter solstice – the day of my surgery. Exactly 6 months later is my annual summer solstice party. How poetic. For those of you who have not attended my summer solstice party, it is a party I started having about 8 years ago when we got our pool and hot tub. I thought it was fitting to celebrate the longest day of the year enjoying our little oasis. At this party I ask all who attend, to plant a flower in my poolside garden. This allows me to think of all my friends, everyday of the summer, while I enjoy the flower they planted. Of course since it is Fitzroy, we enjoy a few drinks and some munchies, go for a swim or a soak in the hot tub and we tell the men that we all dress in white gauze gowns and chant Wiccan incantations to the pagan goddesses! This year June 21st is on a Saturday and I look forward to seeing as many of you as possible on this wonderful day!

Carole

November 30, 2007
Subject: Re: Winter Solstice

Well thank you again for the invitation Carole. Finally you have given me enough time to put together something a little more slimming. And although all the events at these parties sound fabulous, I'm afraid I will have to decline the swimming portion. When wet in a white Wiccan gauze gown, I look like the keel of an over turned boat an inevitably someone calls 911 prompting the coast guard, fire department, swat team and a coroner to show up. And I'm not sure about the planting part either . . . if God had wanted me to bend over, he would have placed diamonds on the ground. I can although, plant my fat, cottage cheese ass in a chair if someone commits to running for my Margaritas. Thanks in advance for the invitation, and let Dan know, I will not be spilling any of the ladies dirty laundry at the Coffee Club the next day.

Cheers,

Patrick

P.S. If need be, and for security purposes only . . . I will send out for a few bitchy drag queens (who couldn't get panty hose in the right size only to be left chaffed) to mark the perimeter. I can assure you that my drag queens can smell a straight virgin man at twenty paces. Let the men be warned about the mating rituals of the infamous "Drag Queen" . . . like a spider, they chew the heads off of the unsuspecting male when they are finished. Any questions? . . . I didn't think so.

LMAO Patrick

December 3, 2007
Subject: Go Fitzroy

Hi Guys,

Well, I half suspected it. Typical political ploy! The councilors have decided that they couldn't possibly close local community centers . . . thus setting the tone for justifying a tax increase . . . whatever. So in the end I do not have to speak in front of city council. Ahhhh, I had all the dramatics planned. Delivering my speech with passion in my voice and at the climax, I inadvertently, accidentally knock the wig off my head revealing the "cancer patient" . . . . LOL . . . I probably spent about 30 hours working on reading the budget end to end, developing arguments and preparing my speech. Am I mad that I don't get to deliver it? No. I am just so happy that I was preoccupied with something other than me for a while. Most therapeutic . . . perhaps they should legislate or at least recommend that all cancer patients do volunteer work! LOL. Anyway, this has renewed my passion in volunteering! All's good.

Carole

December 5, 2007
Subject: Top 10 List

Hi Guys . . . especially the GUYS . . . Girl talk follows - you've been warned LOL!

As the count down to my hysterectomy continues, I decided to share with you my top 10 reasons why it's great to get a hysterectomy:

10. I will no longer have to worry about leakage while I am waiting in a hour long line up to go through customs at Pearson Airport - and having to decide between making my connection or not!
9. I can finally get rid of my "just in case day" grungy underwear.
8. I will no longer have to quietly open the inevitably, squeaky lid to the bin in the washroom at work so as not to alert my co-worker in the next stall that it is "my time of the month!"
7. I will no longer have to count out 25 - 28 days in my blackberry and insert the term "cornflakes" at 7am . . . as was my code for my next period . . . because our calendars are public at work . . . and I did have one man ask me why I have cornflakes in my calendar??!!!!
6. I will only have to wear black pants because I like them, or they make me feel thin, or they suit the occasion rather than

being afraid of ruining the pants of my lime green suit - and then what the hell would I wear with the matching lime green jacket . . . . ?

5. As comes with age, I will never again have to worry about whether my burst of laughter caused an accident . . . or caused an accident!

4. After times worrying about being pregnant, followed by times about worrying about getting pregnant, I will finally be rid of my Achilles heal!

3. I will no longer have to worry about traveling on work trips and long awaited vacations that "just happen to sync up with my time of the month"

2. I will no longer have to worry about waking up in bed so wet from a hot flash that I wonder if I peed the bed (EDIT 6 months later . . . Boy was I wrong about that one LOL)

1. It marks the halfway mark to my full recovery!!!!!!!!!!!!!!

See you soon!

Carole

December 11, 2007
Subject: The other end of the scale

Hi Guys,

A while back I wrote about waiting in at the lab to get my CA125 blood test, and sharing the waiting room with Sir Terrence Matthews, the billionaire! This time I am writing about someone at the other end of the scale.

I went to the Look Good, Feel Better session at the cancer center. Like I say, there is nothing like a trip to the cancer center to be able to see just how lucky I am . . . First of all the Look Good, Feel Better program is a free service put on by the Canadian Cosmetic and Fragrance Association of Canada.

So you may be wondering, why someone, who has never had a facial, nor a pedicure nor a manicure. Someone who spends approximately 10 minutes drying my hair AND applying makeup went to this session.

Well I'll let you in on a little secret . . . I clip coupons, love Canadian Tire money and collect Air Miles too, so do you really think I am going pass up free makeup??? I may not wear too much makeup but if there is even one high-powered wrinkle reducer in the box (Remember I am the one with frickin' zits in my crow's feet!) of makeup we get, I am good to go! We received $500 worth of makeup!

There are 8 ladies sitting in the room. I am again the youngest, but most of these ladies are close to my age and all seem very healthy . . . all is good. I was a bit worried about this being a "downer" session. My wonderful husband is with me . . . by the way he is the FIRST man to go to this session per a lady who has run this for 14 years!!!! What a wonderful sport he is! As you may be able to guess Dan was asked to be the 'model' for the lady showing everyone the different types of wigs and styles. He didn't try them on – instead they had one of the ladies ready to do it. It would have been cute to see Dan with hair!

ahhh . . . I digress, anyway back to my point. One lady shows up late. As soon as she opened the door, you could see her VERY mismatched clothes, very old boots, and what looked like about 5 layers of clothes on her. She took off her hat; her hair was an absolute mess (and that's coming from me LOL) and was falling out. I am convinced she is a street person with every article she owns on her to keep warm and keep them "safe". It was a reminder not only that cancer hits everyone but it also reminded me of how lucky we are to have universal health care! It also reminded me how lucky I am to have a comfortable life, a great job with extra insurance, and enough money to make things comfortable for me. I felt so bad for her I nearly gave her my wig . . . I did take a mental note that I would donate my wig and my other expensive wig that I bought for a Halloween party (. . . guilt . . . .) to the wig lending center at the Ottawa Cancer Center. They lend gently used wigs to women who can't afford to buy one. I think this unfortunate lady is going to try to sell this make up or something.

The session was good – and I imagine wonderful to some ladies who actually spend time really doing their make up – not like the way I do it. I did learn how to do a really good job re-creating my eyebrows . . . for the Fitzroy people – I will **not** be showing

up at Patrick and Tim's party with blue, mega-arched eyebrows!
I also got some tips on stopping my wig from moving up and down
and side to side!

Carole

December 11, 2007
Subject: Re: The Other End of the Scale

Carole, you are so right, we so often don't realize just how much
we have and we take it for granted (Our health included until
something like this comes along.) What you said really made me
think. I let the kids read this, said nothing just wanted them
to think about it and maybe look past there oh soooo hard done
by life (as they see it!) Take care see ya next week

Love Angie

December 11, 2007
Subject: Re: The Other End of the Scale

Wow, you are really seeing a lot that none of us have even thought
about in this big world. You were already such a gifted mind with
many experiences from travel, I can't imagine how "experienced" and
also so "born again" you must feel. Thanks for sharing, really . . . .
as a nurse for many years you have given me many things to think
about that I have not experienced in my career. Thanks.

Happy, happy holidays Carole :-)

Cheryl

December 13, 2007
Re: The Rest is up to you

Hi Guys,

Yesterday, I received an email from my Uncle Bill. My Aunt Maggie
is a 4-year breast cancer survivor. He told me that after her
surgery, her doctor said, "The surgery is 10% of recovery. The

rest is up to you and pointed to his head." I love these words as they make you feel empowered. I read this week in a yoga book about breathing, focus and the power of the mind and I also just read that cancer patients who joined support groups have higher recovery rates. So my creed is: stay positive, full breathing and meditate while focusing on a full recovery and most importantly, keep bugging the crap out of my friends with emails until they beg me to stop or until I have 50,000 words for my book!

I have no need to join a formal support group. I have a built in support group in all of you. As much you have told me you enjoy my emails, I have to admit these emails are for me. They connect me to you and you guys are my living journal. "Living" journal because, how many people have the luxury of ruminating about themselves and then getting such wonderful responses back. That is something a regular journal cannot provide.

For lending me your ears, thanks so much!

Carole

December 15, 2007
Subject: My quilt from Ma Tante Lise, et Agathe

Hi Guys,

What a wonderful gesture. I didn't know about this – until I was diagnosed. When you are diagnosed with cancer, someone may ask for a quilt to be made for you. When I was diagnosed, Dan's Aunt Lise put my name in for a quilt. (Lise just finished going through her own bout with cancer and is doing great.)

Agathe, is the wife of Vace, one of our coffee club regulars and she happens to be the person who makes the quilts for people with cancer in our area! I am truly blessed to have someone ask that a quilt be made for me but also to actually know the person who made and quilted it.

Thank you ladies, It is already a cherished item that keeps me warm.

Carole

December 17, 2007
Subject: It's all in the movies . . .

Hi Guys,

After almost 40cm of snow yesterday, it was rise and shine for my
pre-op appointment at the General. Of course it was at 8am. With
over a 100km drive, getting up at 5:45 was not fun. With the left
over snow removal still ongoing, we wanted to be safe. Even with
a stop at our new favorite east end Timmy's we made it to the
hospital by 7:45. All the traditional questions regarding health
insurance, desire for semi private or private room etc. already
sorted out by phone last week, today was to be 2-3 hours, I was
told, giving blood and talking to the anesthesiologist. I fill
out a few forms (apparently other than this cancer thing I am in
fabulous health!!) I feel it is only necessary to mention that I
only drink 2 - 3 drinks a week - they did not seem to care about
the spacing . . . and after writing down that I quit smoking 2.5
years ago I feel I don't need to mention a few drags at the party
last weekend . . . at least not in writing.

After the forms, Dan and I make our way to a room smaller than
most people's ground floor half bathroom! A nurse joins us. Two
things here are worth mentioning. First of all I find it very
interesting that they are now asking patients what vitamins and
herbs they are taking - in case of conflict or contra-indications
with surgery or meds. This is encouraging that the ground swell
of people supplementing traditional medicine with natural medicine
must be big enough to warrant the questioning. Personally I have
come prepared with my 12 bottles of "herbs and spices" (for some
of you . . . that is one more herb than KFC's traditional recipe
chicken :-) I had already read about some of them that should
be stopped prior to surgery, but with my worse than ever short
term memory I had forgotten which one was bad to take . . . .
so last Friday I had stopped taking all but my multi-vitamin,
vitamin C and B Complex. The nurse didn't flinch at any of my 12
supplements except the Milk Thistle . . . she had not heard of
that one before. She listed them all - the list did not fill up
all the lines allocated on the form - so there must be people
more obsessed about this then me. I then pull out the recipe for

my green drink . . . the only wince is over the Sheep sorrel. I tell her it is a herb and she gives it her blessing . . . perhaps I will stop that one just for the week.

She then proceeds to tell me about the 3 different types of anesthesia options . . . I use the word options loosely as I am sure I really don't have a choice - but just in case I am ready to discuss my love of Demerol over morphine. She tells me there are locals, general and epidural. I am, of course familiar with all of these options having had an epidural when I had my C-Section and remember vividly the smell of my own flesh burning as they cauterized something down there. Then she hits me! Worse than the wig lady! You'll be getting an epidural. A sudden wave of nausea hits me, the box we are sitting in shrinks, the lights seem extraordinarily bright, I look up at Dan who is standing in the corner by the door . . . . the pitch and volume of my voice rises "I'm going to be awake when they do the surgery?!" "No, no no, the epidural is for after surgery so you can get up and walk better." My heart slows down to a regular beat and I am pretty sure my "near faint" level drop in blood pressure is back to normal.

There is a lot more talk about pain and graphic details about surgery. With all the strength I have shown with the Chemo treatment, the converse seems to be true about the surgery . . . I realize I really don't like the thought of this . . . oh well suck it up and get 'er done!

Next I am on to the Anesthesiologist. She introduces herself asks about any allergies, I quickly mention my slight indiscretion with a few drags and she smiles that it's okay. I mention that I seem to puke with morphine she assures me - most women do. She tells me they have medicine to counter morphine nausea and other pain relievers as well . . . I forget the name now but some of you have mentioned it to me in the past. I tell her about my allergy to sulfa based drugs and am willing to tell her my entire life history . . . instead I just tell her "do a good job, do a good job" doing my best Steve Buscemi impersonation - from Armageddon - I know he was talking about disarming a nuclear missile on a rogue asteroid hurtling toward earth destined to destroy the planet, when he said it in the movie, but hey to me there are parallels!

The other visit I had today was from a white coated person . . . not sure of her title . . . asking me again if I would donate my tumor to research, I told her I had already agreed, but she told me this was for a new study. They are doing tissue testing – injecting a virus into tumors that they believe will kill the tumor! Of course I agree – I will have to follow up on this one. It seems akin to the "if you can't beat 'em join 'em" philosophy . . . I wonder did somebody get sick with a virus by accident and stumble onto this or did some doctor think of this while "wasted" watching *War of the Worlds* and thought of this as the big aliens fell to one of our earthly viruses? So I sign. As we are driving home it occurs to me. Somewhere in the city there is room . . . hot? Cold? Filled with Petri dishes full of tumors being kept alive so that some researcher can attempt to kill them with a virus . . . sounds like an opportunity for a John Carpenter movie or Stephen King novel!

I go in on Friday but I don't get a time until Thursday night. I'll tell Dan to make sure he brings in my blackberry so I can send you guys email while I am recovering!

Talk to you later in the week!

Carole

December 17, 2007
Subject: RE: It's all in the movies . . .

Man your heart must have really stopped when you thought you would be awake . . . YIKES . . . I must say I had to look up sheep sorrel . . . Sounds like something all of us might want to be taking:
"Sheep sorrel was considered the most active herb in Essiac for stimulating cellular regeneration, **detoxification** and cleansing". Carole, take care of yourself, and soon you will be done with this nasty interruption of your wonderful life. Thinking, of you.

Cheers,

Deb

December 17, 2007
Subject: RE: It's all in the movies . . .

Hey Carole,

You have been on my mind so much lately. Watching that storm yesterday, I was thinking, what if someone like Carole had to be at a hospital in the middle of a massive storm like this. I guess you just cope, and plan for any emergency! No different than having babies in the dead of winter and having to start cars in the middle of the night, and the temperature is − 50! What fond memories, of those, almost 14 years ago. It makes you stronger . . . and planning skills really come into play.

So I just wanted to tell you that you are constantly in my prayers (I talk to Him even more during Advent, so you timed it right!), and will be even more so starting Thursday night, Friday and the weekend. I wanted to tell you that your cancer has helped me put very many things into perspective throughout this hectic "getting ready for Christmas" season. When I am rushing around shopping, being pulled in many directions for Christmas dinner plans, obsessing over stocking stuffers for nieces and nephews, telling my son that "Santa" probably won't be able to deliver a Gas-powered go cart with a 4-stroke engine, I find myself always stopping and just offering up a prayer for your health, and what you must be going through with your "preparations".

Anyway, stay brave, and courageous, and above all, funny. Your perspective and sense of humour is contagious, and I just wanted you to know that.

Tell Dan (or if you are up to it) to be sure to send out an email over the weekend with an update. Let us know if you are up for any visitors (as long as a major storm doesn't get in the way!). I'll come & lull you to sleep with boring stories of work (better than any anesthetic to numb your mind).

Talk to you soon,

Mo

December 19, 2007
Subject: My darkest hour

Hi Guys, I couldn't send this email out - I just wrote it.

Well, here is something unexpected. I have been overwhelmed with a sense of dread. I don't know why, but I have this feeling that I will not survive my surgery. At Brian and Cathy's Christmas party, I felt like I was at my funeral, most of my friends were there, everyone was dressed in black and I wasn't. It was such a weird sensation and such an overwhelming fear. I did not sleep that night. I have been so uptight since then. No matter how hard I try to shake it, it keeps nagging at me. Perhaps I am just afraid of the anesthetic. I don't know, but it can't be good going into this operation with such dread.

Today Sherri came by to perform Reiki on me. It turned out to be such a cathartic session. Aside from opening up about these deepest, darkest concerns, that I felt I couldn't share with anyone for fear of upsetting everyone around me, we ceremoniously burned the magazine where I inadvertently read stats on survival rates on my type of cancer. I cried. I worked through my concerns. I will never know if such dread was required, however I do know that I feel balanced once again, positive and only slightly worried about the surgery. This I can manage.

Thanks Sherri!

Carole

December 19
Subject: House Fire In Fitzroy

Hi Friends,

If you haven't already heard, there was a house in Fitzroy Harbour that burnt down last evening (up the hill). I'm told that it was a complete loss. The family included one female adult and two children. I met with Caroline (Principal of St. Michael's) this morning and they have things in full swing to help out the family.

The school is asking for donations of clothing, blankets, food or cash donations for a female child aged 6, a boy 13 and a female parent described as small to medium in size. All donations are being received at St. Michael's School here in Fitzroy.

There was no mention of Christmas gifts, but I'm sure it wouldn't hurt either. If you are in the position to help please do so as soon as possible, it's not getting any warmer out there.

Patrick

December 20
Subject: Tears All Day

Hi Guys,

Tears 1

First of all thanks to all of you who came out to my house and sang Christmas Carols. Please pass this on to anyone who is not on my regular email list. Your support and love shone through your voices. You brought me and Josh to tears and touched the hearts of Dan and Noella. Thanks so much. Thanks for the wonderful quilt, for wearing my colour ribbon and for being here for me!

What a wonderful place to live and what wonderful friends in my "box of chocolates"

Tears 2

Yesterday, everyone in Fitzroy came together again for the family that lost their house in the fire Tuesday night. I pulled together some toys and stuff and a few sweaters for the mom, some of my Look Good/Feel Good "cancer" makeup and toiletries and a new pair of PJs that I had been given by someone when they found out I have cancer . . . I figure this poor lady has nothing new and I can wear some of my old PJs. This is a case where "re-gifting" is acceptable - especially if my cancer can benefit someone! The donations are pouring in and the community is rising to the occasion again! I happened to drop my stuff at the school right when the local news was there. So I was on the news. They interviewed

me . . . I started to choke up . . . I missed it on TV last night.
CJOH is the most popular news cast in Ottawa . . . there's now a
lot of people out there who think I'm a crier . . . to you guys
at work . . . I don't really cry all that much . . . gotta keep
that image up ;-)

I am so proud of Josh he went to his room, found a whole bunch of
toys including XBOX games and his old XBOX console and donated
them to the family across the street instead of selling them or
trading them for new games.

Tears 3

I had my first Reiki session yesterday. It was very cathartic . . .
and humbling as I realize I am not Wonder Woman, Xena warrior
princess, nor Laura Croft . . . despite having past photographic
evidence from Halloween parties that say otherwise! I had a wonderful
cry, ceremoniously burned an article I accidentally read with
some numbers on cancer I didn't want to read. Instead I choose
strength, belief and faith . . . I have been a little nervous
about my surgery . . . again an admission of weakness. (This is
big for me guys LOL!) I think the Reiki cleared my head . . . and
my near obsessive worrying about my surgery. I had been wondering
why I hadn't been told to take an enema or anything prior to my
surgery. This morning I called my surgeon and was quickly told
I needed to drink a disgusting concoction of sodium phosphate
oral solution and water . . . AVOID THIS AT ALL COSTS!! It is
supposed to clear the bowels but it nearly made me puke! Anyway,
I am glad that I called. Had I not, my surgery may have had to
be cancelled or worse. It reminds me again, as we are all human
so each of us must take on a level of responsibility for our own
health and believe in our gut instinct.

Irony 1

I got a phone call yesterday. It was a telemarketer telling me
about a unique insurance - just for women - protection for certain
female diseases including cancer. I quickly alerted the woman that
I already have ovarian cancer. This stopped her short. First time
I have ever stifled a telemarketer without resorting to hanging up
the phone. I am however still entered in the draw to win a trip
for two to the Mediterranean!

After a tearful, wonderful day yesterday I must quickly sign off, as I fear the sodium phosphate has taken effect!

Real quickly . . . this morning I met the lady whose house burned down, for the first time, at the store . . . she was wearing one of my sweaters . . . my heart is full – this is what Christmas is about. This is why Fitzroy Harbour is so special!

I plan on being back on line on Saturday . . . I apologize in advance if my message is garbled, has more typos and contains more swear words than usual . . . it'll be just because of the morphine or hopefully Demerol!

Carole

December 20, 2007
Subject: RE: Tears All Day

You are amazing . . . and thankfully telling my story without me
having to tell it. I am truly moved by the way you write and the
way you put this awful disease into a real life story that I so
can relate to. The word sodium phosphate still makes me gag . . .
I have to go for another colonoscopy in the new year and I don't
have any idea how I'm going to drink that putrid stuff without
puking . . . which by the way I do as soon as I drink the second
one . . . yuck, I might have to puke right now.

I am sending out positive vibes, positive prayers and positive
thoughts . . . all in the direction of Fitzroy Harbour, so if the
ground shakes it's just me. You are well and will be even more
perfect after your surgery.

Big Hugs . . . to you and Dan and Josh (even though I don't know
Josh and my guess is he wouldn't really want a big hug from me,
but I'm sending it anyway . . .)

I will wait to hear how your surgery goes, but I already know
that it's going to go great and that you are well.

Take care, my friend,
Dianne

December 20, 2007
Subject: RE: Tears All Day

Thanks Dianne. All my friends have been my "rocks". Having gone
through this experience yourself – you are my pillar!

Truly thanks!!!

Carole

December 20, 2007
Subject: RE: Tears All Day

XENA,

With the Reiki, yoga, and healthful ingestion of the best nature
has to offer, let it rest that you have done your part this far
and the crying is just part of the healing. I have learned more
about you in the past several weeks and your emotional side is
never a weakness, but completes you. I hope you and I can get
to know each other more over the years to come. Seems we have
both held back a little on sharing "warmth with one another" you
are my sister-in-law and I care more about all 3 of you that I
have ever let you know . . . for fear that you would think I was
weak . . . stupid humans we are. I was hoping to see you tonight,
but we are quarantined AGAIN, and not worth it for sure to expose
any of you. You live in the best little town I have ever seen and
not a single person in West Carleton that knows you will not be
with you in spirit tomorrow. Love to you and talk to you "over
the phone" at Christmas.

Heather

PS Your Halloween costume as Xena was appropriate!

December 21, 2007
Subject: Carole McCaskill Update 5pm

Carole's surgery was over around 1:30 to 2:00 pm. She has been
in the recovery room until about 10 minutes ago. Carole is now
resting in her room with a little pain but nothing she can't
manage "says Carole." She did say that, "the surgeon was cute."
Tim spent most of the afternoon with Dan at the hospital and is
now on his way home . . . be prepared, she is drugged with a
blackberry in tow. We could here from her soon.

Patrick

Hi Readers, In editing this, I have decided that I am not editing
some of the emails I sent out . . . especially when I was using my
Blackberry (with a very tiny keyboard) and while on Benadryl . . .
they are much more amusing . . . so bear with the errors and
enjoy! I will put a little (Blackberry/Benadryl Alert) beside
unedited mails.

Blackberry/Benadryl alert!

December 22, 2007
Subject: Up and Running

Hi Guys,

Nevery have I felt so much guilt for drinking a lemon herbal tea.
I had some on my way in for surgery . . . apparently sipping
herbal tea with nothing in it. Appatently hhoney herbal eas is NOT
included in the clear liquid category! Doh! Dan was right again.
Things went well – I asked the OR team to make sure my tattoo
didn't end up becoming a diastorted Chinese swear "character"
when they made the incision! My tattoo "area" is still covered
by bandages so I will have to report later on it.

The team of doctors an intern s, 3rd year med students and nurses
lead by the ruggedly handsome Dr. Faught (calm down Patrick, he's
not McDreamy or McSte4amy but he is cute!) Did a great job. Dr.

Faught said it was "the best possible scenario"!!! There was no fluid, the chemo really worked to shink it right down, nothing in my lymph nodes!!! And just small microscopic spots in my abdomen cavity, the size of grains of sand! I was go bon the (ok nurses – this close to the name . . .) perintonatal??? Catheter inserted for future chemo injections.

Thanks to all of you for all your support, good vibes, for calling on the angels, green and white chakras and prayers! They say it takes a village to raise a child well it also takes a village to beat this and we are winning!

Love to you all,

Carole

December 22, 2007
Subject: RE: Up and Running

This will be a **VERY** merry Christmas for all the McCaskill family. I am so very pleased to hear your good news, Carole.

Now – follow what the doctors tell you and be a good patient. And remember – Dan **is** right!

Thinking of you,

Patricia

December 22, 2007
Re: Pain pump 30 times in an hour!

Hi Guys,

I received my "drug report" this morning. Apparently I hit the drug pump 30 times in one hour!
So basically I have to refer back to my first chemo treatment . . .
We Harbourites can handle or think we can handle our drinks, or in this case "a cousin" of morphine. Like a good party in Fitzroy, apparently I was not fully aware of time between doses. Luckily,

drugs given at hospitals are more regulated then at a party in
the Harbour and the self-regulated pump allows only 4 hits an
hour. LOL! The nurse kept asking my pain level while laying still
and I would tell her four on a scale of ten. She thought maybe I
should use the pump less since I was making myself nauseous - no
comments!
There is a lesson here - not sure but it seems to have something
to do with too much, too quickly - causing nausea - I think that
might be it!

Carole

December 28, 2007
Re: Staples, Staplers and Bracelets

Hi Guys,

After a week of holding my gut when anticipating a sneeze, cough, hiccup, or God forbid - throwing up, (which I didn't do) I can report that the city must have been busy out paving the Carp road, the 417, Alta Vista and Smyth Roads because the trip back to the General Hospital for my staple removal was nowhere near as painful as it was driving home on Christmas Eve! LOL! It is amazing the difference even 5 days of recovery can make. Aside from feeling totally helpless over the holidays, they were wonderful and we managed to do many of our family traditions with some modification. Aside from an untimely bout of nausea right as Christmas dinner was being served (no food with my pain medication = doh!) all went well.

As one would expect everything in life takes on greater significance when you are fighting cancer and no time more so than Christmas. It has been an awakening of emotions both happy and sad and always reflective. It has solidified something I always knew intellectually and now emotionally and can truly empathize with, the millions of people in the world less fortunate than us. I am not even talking about the 3rd world. I am talking about those next door or down the road that are alone. Next Christmas I will be giving my time. More so then ever it has become glaringly true that the giving of our time IS unequivocally more precious than the giving a dollar. Sorry I am preaching I am going to blame it on the mood swings of menopause coupled with the holidays and I might even pull out the cancer card on this one.

Anyway Dan has decided to keep my staples, which were pulled out by a wonderful nurse who grew up only a few blocks from Dan. He seems to think Carol & Ted can turn them into a Devine Creation bracelet or something. We'll have to get them cleaned first and pull them out of the "biohazard Ziploc bag!" I'm not sure if he intends for me, or him to wear it but hey, who said Dan and I were normal!

Also I found out from my nurse today that not only is Dr. Faught cute and nice - he is apparently the head of the entire Women's health department for the Ottawa Hospital. Nice!

I am not sure what Dan thought the removal of the staples would be like, but when he saw that it wasn't a major procedure he did state that "MJ could have done this" but I quickly told him that I have entrusted MJ with many things in my life but after the infamous stapler charades incident I was afraid of the size of the staple remover she would have used! LOL! For those who have never heard that story, MJ acted out stapler so badly in charades we all thought she was doing an alligator, crocodile or some other large mouthed man-eater!?!

Anyway, there are only a few grains of sand size cancer left in my abdomen. I begin a 24-hour dose of chemo around the 3rd week of January. For the first time in months my dream last night was about returning to work and having to kick out the person who is filling in for me while I am off! This is a big thing to dream of the future. A cured me! I am so glad there is so little left but you know how hard it is to clean up those last few grains of sand so I look forward to all your support in 2008. One lesson I knew, but have also come to fully appreciate, is the fabulous friends and support system I have. I am truly blessed!

Thank you,

Carole

December 28, 2007
Subject: Re: Staples, Staplers and Bracelets

Good Morning Carole,

I was so happy to come into work this morning to find your emails.
I am pleased to hear your humour coming through so strongly in
your e-mail.

Mary Jo and the STAPLER have provided us with many laughs over
the years, today I was especially appreciative of the visual!

I can hardly wait to see the Jewelry!

Glad to hear you are feeling less pain. You are an incredible
woman and friend Carole.

I wish you much laughter, love and especially great health in 2008.
My positive energy, and requests on your behalf, will continue
indefinitely.

I love you dearly Carole. A great 2008 awaits us!

Love to Dan and Josh.

Lots of love,

Sally xoxoxo

December 31, 2007
Subject: 525600

525600 minutes, that's how I measure this year.
Through teardrop, laughter, joy and love.
That's how I measure this year.

Tear drops-the day my sister told me she had cancer & the day my
dog Harley was hit by a car

Laughter – a day at Cedar Point with my sister, laughing so hard after a ride on the rollercoaster and a night of reminiscing of days gone by.

Joy – Christmas day with my family, knowing that everything was going to be okay! We as a family and a community were going to win this fight with cancer. – Looking back at a year with so many other things to give thanks for.

Love – Family and friends

That is how I measure this year.

Just one more thing and that is how proud I am of you! You are so strong and so very lucky to have sooooo many people that care and love you. You are amazing. Here is to 2008! Bring it on. Happy New Year! Cheers!

Love Ya

Angie

January 2, 2008
Subject: Wonderful New Year's

Hi Brian and Cathy,

Thanks so much for hosting New Year's dinner. I couldn't have asked for a more perfect evening! The food was fabulous and the company was terrific.

Thank you for such a wonderful evening, Rob, Sonya, Ken, Judy, Gwen, Rick, Patrick and Tim, We enjoyed it. A little less rowdy than some years! I appreciate that it was kept low key (no crazy drinking, dancing and late night partying) just for me!

Carole

January 5, 2008
Re: What a difference a little hair makes

Hi Guys,

Well it has been about 6 weeks since my last round of chemo, two since my surgery. My abdomen feels good. I still have to be a little cautious . . . or I will have to face the wrath of Dan ;-) I do have to be careful with the snowy conditions outside. I am sure slipping now would set me back a little! I feel so good today I signed up for my yoga again. Although I will just go and breathe for the first couple of weeks. I am anxious to be able to go out and walk again.

My hair is actually starting to grow back (some of it I never lost and it is longer and I also just started to notice a distinct "hairline" starting to form along my forehead yippee! This is encouraging however I do have to remember I am going back in for 3 more rounds and my hairline will probably regress again. Perhaps it will be less since they are injecting the chemo directly into my abdomen and contorting my body in half to help keep it in my mid section, and it may not circulate as much through my blood system??? I will have to ask and report on that later in the month.

Believe it or not when you sit in the same spot for much of the day looking out the window you notice minor changes – the good news – the days are getting longer!

I am feeling very good about a few things I have read lately, including a report in "Consumer Report on Health" akin to the regular Consumer Reports but – on health matters – with no advertising to sway its perspective. My first issue had an article on the emerging believe that there is a connection between salt/sugar and cancer. So much so that the government is considering putting restrictions on the amount of sodium manufacturers' can use in their products . . . I am sure that is many years from now! Anyway, it does back up my very salt/sugar restricted diet I have been on since this all started.

I also just read some information on chemicals that cause cancer in lab rats that are in cosmetics and body products etc . . . I remember the scare several years ago about aluminum in deodorant. I think I will have a go at wearing no makeup a bit of a try. Although, with my extremely scarce eyebrows and lashes I think I may wait on ditching the mascara and eyebrow pencil – they have become my new best friends!

This reading supports my theories that I can help with my recovery in tangible ways!

By the way, since someone asked . . . between 2 days of fasting, removal of my "women" parts and more, 3 days on Jell-O, broth and juice I lost 6 pounds – so I figure a couple pounds of it was "me". I have been very good over the holidays . . . I did sneak 3 Ferrero Roche chocolates, one butter tart, a couple of short bread cookies and a couple handfuls of chips – heck its Christmas. As for my, shall we call it "unique" weight loss plan, I think I need to assume at least 2 pounds of sweat have lead to the 6 pound loss . . . man these hot flashes or night sweats make Niagara Falls look tame. Thank God I'm bald . . . my head would be twice as hot if I wasn't. I have 3 pillows that I have to rotate out every couple of hours at night, as they get soaked. I had been experiencing peri-menopausal hot flashes – now with full out post hysterectomy hot flashes, I am ready to start the warm soya milk my doctor recommended about a year ago, I am thinking of popping open the bottles of Red Clover and Black Cohosh that my *Living with Menopause* – prep reading material suggested I try for hot flashes, but alas it is going to have to take a full fledged flood of sweat before I give up my caffeine!

The first PGA event was on TV this weekend, days are getting longer – tempting us to believe spring is just around the corner. West Carleton Football meetings are starting up, we are in the middle of a January thaw, I fit my bathing suit better than last year, I feel very good, hell even my hot flashes are good – when I consider that I just read about sweating out toxins! My stomach muscles are quickly recovering, I started working on Trivia questions and using my new Taylor Made rac pitching wedge in a round of golf is not too far off. I have a wonderful family, friends and community making this journey much easier than many others in my shoes and I have re-discovered my love of writing and have a whole audience of friends willing to read my musings.

Thanks Guys - here's to 2008!

Carole

January 13, 2008

Dear Josh,

I have been contemplating writing you letters. Finally with a little nudge from a very wise man, (Thanks Gilles) I have decided that writing you a letter is in sync with who I am and will not bring on a bad outcome nor is it an ominous omen. I had been contemplating writing you "letters" for some time - well before my diagnosis, as I realized that the beauty of the written word is that it allows one time to carefully formulate the message, carefully choose the perfect words to express your feelings and eliminates the wild card of an "interjection" that can lead you down a different path. I suppose that is why MSN, emails and texting have become so popular. As you enter your teen years, both Dad and I realize that we will have less influence on you, as friends quickly become your number one source of "approval". My hope for you is that you can find a balance between remaining true to whom you are, with the teen dilemma of having to conform and fit into the "norm". Try to find a balance between fun and study, breaking away and finding you, to going to far. Although you may not like it Dad and I have a role to play in this delicate dance. We are there to act as an appropriate level of resistance, a little impedance to slow you down a bit along the way. I hope you can appreciate this role as we can understand your need to "breakaway" it is part of the growing up process, it is natural and I believe we will all get through this without too much trouble - since we have such a strong trust and respect for you and you for us. Always feel free to talk to us. You know both Dad and I have been there - I didn't talk to my parents as much as I should have and that is

too bad for me and was my doing. Remember you can ask, hear the
response and decide how much of it to absorb . . .

Love you,

Mom

January 14, 2008
Subject: Okay now I'm scared

Hi Guys,

Tomorrow I head to the cancer clinic to find out details about
my next Chemo treatment using the catheter. (I will send out a
follow up on that one!) But that's not the scary part!!

I did get a call today from a psychologist. Apparently everyone on
this trial needs to see a psychologist. There is long questionnaire
to fill out. I am very curious. I have spent many hours on self-
reflection. I think it's mandatory when you have a life threatening
illness but I am not sure ;-) . . . although I can verify that out
of a sample size of two - it is ha-ha! But now they want to know
how I feel about a lot of things. I'm not so sure they need me to
fill out a questionnaire to know that I am scared, concerned and
sometimes sad - I may be optimistic but I am not super woman. At
least it is a questionnaire . . . I have discovered - as MOST of
you have . . . that I am much more expressive about my feelings
in the written word then I am verbally.

It is quit ironic that I feel so happy about so much in my life
right now . . . is this typical - I assume so but what do I know? I
will fill out the form . . . I only hope they will tell me if I am
a 'normal' cancer patient or not . . . I tend to think I am not. I
believe I am more positive than most, more proactive than many, and
maybe, just maybe luckier than some! So far everything has gone well
and as the Shakespeare said "Out dam spot out!" (You know the sand
size spots left in my abdomen.) Just a few more treatments to go!

Talk to you soon . . . I will definitely follow up on the psychology
"questionnaire".

Carole

January 15, 2008
Subject: The Captain and periToneal

Hi Guys,

I went in for my post op appointment. As always let me start
with an observation. It is sad to say that the cancer clinic is
absolutely packed and appointments are running one hour behind.
All around me I see sad faces. I lean over to Dan and tell him I
don't like coming here. Luckily this is only my second appointment
here. All my other appointments are up on the 8th floor of the
General and somehow the small room that only fits 8 women seems
much less daunting.

While waiting, I pick up a *McLean's* magazine, which has an article
on the recent "Guardacil Vaccine" that our government has approved
for girls as young as 9. I am mortified as I read about the lack
of long term clinical trials, the concern over whether or not
the vaccine will stay effective for 20 years . . . the amount
of time required (at minimum) when given to a girl as young as
nine. I am aghast that 9 years olds get the green light for the
vaccine after the short-term trials so far were only carried out
on 100 nine-year-old girls and followed for only 18 months. Not
to mention that I am mortified to hear that several young girls
have died and company officials are saying the line "there is
not enough scientific evidence to support a direct connection".
Statements like that always put my guard up. Top that off with the
fact that our current test for cervical cancer (your yearly PAP
smear) is very effective, rates of cervical cancer in Canada are
very low and add the fact that Guardacil only guards against two
forms of HPV. My point, to all my friends with young daughters,
for my part I say, pray for abstinence as long as possible,
teach about condoms, and take her for yearly PAP smears, and
wait until they know a little bit more about the vaccine and its
long term effects on pre-pubescent girls . . . hold off until
they are at least midway through their teens. Sorry – just my
two cents . . .

Anyway back to my appointment. Part of my appointment was to
get my pathology report. It turns out I have peritoneal cancer.
Basically it is in the ovarian cancer family but it originated
in my abdomen not in my ovaries.

My prognosis and treatment are the same but when they operated they found no sign of cancer in my ovaries or my uterus. All they found was scaring on my omentum. The Surgical Oncologist, Dr. Webber-Pals, the female on the team (darn I was hoping to get another peek at Dr. Faught!) said that NOT finding any cancer is always the best possible scenario – which the nurse had said I had none left. As with ovarian cancer, it can come back, and Dr Faught had said there were grains of sand left. Either way I still get 3 more rounds of chemo. Apparently I responded exceptionally well to the chemo! (Couple that with good eating, positive thinking and a great support network – things have gone great so far!!)

These next 3 rounds are through a peritoneal catheter (to treat my peritoneal cancer – seems apropos!) They stick a needle into the round disk attached to my ribs (under the skin) and inject the chemo into the catheter over 2 hours. Then they lift my legs to keep it in my abdomen, roll me from side to side . . . someone in the room mentioned something about using a spit to ensure I was well basted all over, they give me saline to salt me up and with my regular nightly hot flashes I should be well baked by the next morning!

In the information they gave me it mentioned concerns over kidney problems (it is tough on the kidneys to manage cleaning out the toxins) so I asked the nurse what I could take to "help" keep my kidneys healthy (thinking diet or vitamins) she laughed and said that at each chemo appointment they take reading of kidney "efficiency" she said typically the number is "40" not sure what that meant but the number was "40" and mine was at 120. Apparently my kidneys are very, very efficient – I took the opportunity to point out to Dan that there finally is a pay off for putting up with all the pee stops on long trips!

The information they gave me also said to wear loose fitting pants. So I ask the nurse "how loose". I told her that my pants fit me 4 days prior to going to "Emergency" and having 4 liters of fluid drained from my abdomen . . . the nurse said they are only putting in 2 liters of fluid. That was good enough to tell me how loose my pants need to be. It also gives me a heads up as to how much my eating, breathing and other bodily functions will be impacted. If I recall I was still golfing and just a little slow, eating ok but feeling a bit full after eating and going to the bathroom more than normal. I assume it is only for a week or two until it gets absorbed into my blood stream and peed out. I can handle that!

A week after my overnight "Shake and Bake" stay I go in for my day chemo treatment. So, more time spent at the hospital but all worth while. I feel extremely positive about the report I got today. Again I thank all of you for your prayers, thoughts and support.

More to come soon!

Carole

January 17, 2008
Re: Late Night Musings . . .

Hi Guys,

So I have been thinking about peritoneal cancer. It's a rare form of cancer, in the ovarian cancer family, but in the abdomen. How did it start in my omentum? Here's what I am thinking. When I was going through In Vitro Fertilization, it was determined that my right fallopian tube was covered in adhesions. So every second month (we release an egg from one ovary a month, typically back and forth from the left to the right side) upon leaving my ovary, my egg would not be able to find its way down the fallopian tube and would 'wander' around my abdomen . . . ultimately being 'reabsorbed' back into my body . . . one might assume into my omentum, since it is a layer of fat that protects the lower abdomen. Seems like a logical explanation to me.

So now I am wondering if this is too simple or if this is something that cancer researchers have already looked at?? I start thinking about eggs in general . . . how they only last so long. What does that mean exactly? Chicken eggs in the fridge eventually go bad, and ultimately get rotten. Rotten things in the fridge turn green and the green starts to multiple and spread very quickly to other food items beside them. Is this what is happening to our eggs?

Then I begin to think about my hot flashes and night sweats — which I have been having for a while on and off? Was this cancer simply a matter of a few rotten eggs from my 'fridge' that's on the blink – heating up and starting to break? And in my case, the egg carton is broken and the rotten eggs are spreading to the butter beside the eggs? Could it be that basic? Then I start thinking about my In Vitro Fertilization. After "super ovulation" where 13 eggs matured in one cycle they inserted a tube, and 'aspirated' the eggs. Could we not aspirate our old rotting eggs from women who are beyond the years of wanting children and remove the risk of the rotten eggs from even developing? No surgery at all?

These are all questions that should not be rattling around in my brain at 3am in the morning. These seem more like the type of 'deep logical' thinking from a night out partying . . . not the type of thinking I experience dead sober. Perhaps I can chalk it up to "Chemo Brain" (thanks for that term Sarah) . . . bad short term memory, heightened awareness of just about everything and perhaps "fuzzy logic" LOL.

I must remember to run this theory by the team at the cancer clinic next Tuesday. Perhaps I am on to something ;-)

Carole

January 17, 2008
Subject: software bugs . . . a cancer research
analogy?

Hi Guys,

When we encounter a software bug, sometimes we are lucky we can see exactly where the code is wrong. Unfortunately at other times the code was written years ago, perhaps in Pascal, instead of C++, perhaps the designer has left and he was lax at documenting his design. Sometimes the problem is systemic; it has tentacles out to thousands of lines of code. These are the difficult bugs to fix. Sometimes we are lucky and we can find the root cause. Sometimes we say the problem was already in the code and we make sure we haven't made it worse. Sometimes only one or two people complain and we put it on the back burner. When a systemic bug bubbles to the surface and there is enough pressure to fix it, sometimes we find a fix. It doesn't address the root cause but we fix it and test it. It fixes the problem, at least temporarily. Sometimes the same problems bubbles up in a different line of code, sometimes the fix creates a new bug or the same bug manifested itself in a slightly different manner. These bugs are often complex because they are nestled in 'spaghetti' code and are very complex to untwine. Multiple engineers with multiple areas of expertise wrote all these thousands of lines of code. Hours and hours of analysis are required to try to find the root cause of the bug and put an end to the ever-mounting bug reports. Sometimes it is just easier, faster and more profitable to find a band-aid solution to fix the immediate bug being raised rather then finding the root cause.

This is how I feel we are treating cancer. Not only is it more profitable to treat cancer but it is easier . . . in many ways since there are many 'suspected' cancer causing agents in our food, health care products, make-up and cleaning products. Removing these carcinogens, forcing people and companies to change, costs money. This is a hard nut to swallow for a company especially without a definitive reason or parity across an industry, between countries. Thanks to tough environmental legislation in Europe all lead has been removed from my company's products. This was at tremendous expense and 'lost opportunity'. I can understand why such activities are tough undertakings for some companies. To me I am proud that my company has done something about lead content. Was it an altruistic decision? Not likely. However, I do like to believe that the environment and ultimately our health was a contributing factor. I think we need our government to act, to take a stand to help prevent cancer.

Carole

January 18, 2008
Re: Bring on the Heat!

Hi Guys,

Since mid September I have had a hot bath in Epsom salts at least 5 nights a week. On top of that I have gone to bed every night with a hot water bottle. I had read that cancer cells don't like heat. Plus I found it comforting initially when I had the fluid and digestive issues. That's a hot water bottle every night throughout my entire treatment. I keep telling Dan as well that we need to get out in the hot tub – as soon as the weather gets a bit better (I don't want to push it in the cold weather with my immunity down during chemo) I see lots of hot tub parties in our future! Also, lots of trips down south to get out of the cold weather! As per Dr. Christine Northrup on *Oprah* yesterday, she said that night sweats is the body's way of trying to rid itself of toxins . . . based on that I am happy to keep waking up in the middle of the night drenched in sweat!

Anyway, I saw a quick clip on TV yesterday, where they discussed a new treatment. Basically it is the inter-peritoneal chemotherapy that I get next Tuesday – only they heat up the Chemo "cocktail". I will have to ask them if they are heating it up for me . . . I think I am going to take my hot water bottle – just in case! Between my theories and everything else . . . man they are going to hate me LOL.

Carole

January 22, 2008
Subject: Criminal Minds – BAU

Hi Guys,

For those who don't follow the TV show Criminal Minds, BAU is Behavioral Analysis Unit. Last night I felt like I was part of the show . . . I filled out the forms from the psychologist.
As I am checking off the applicability of statements – to my personality – I keep recognizing the fact that most of these questions are looking for signs of things like bi-polar disease, OCD, psychosis and I am sure a plethora of other 'disorders'.

"Of course I don't think someone is planting thoughts in my head!" I answer "false." Whew, I think I got that one correct! Next question, "do you think you will be famous one day?" Ewwww, this is a little harder. I answer that one "somewhat true". Next question "do you feel you have thoughts that are genius?" Again I answer somewhat true. But wait in my defense, if that psychologist had read my email on the "heat" effects on cancer, or my untrained

theories on how ovarian cancer gets into the omentum to cause
peritoneal cancer – she might agree!!?! LOL. And if she knew I was
writing a book she may not diagnose me with having "delusions of
grandeur! Right? After a moment of trepidation I realize I will
need to qualify my answers when I speak to her.

I finish filling out the forms and again the only stumbling block is
with the question "has drinking ever gotten you into trouble?" I
feel this is ambiguous. What is her definition of trouble? Police, job
issues or oops I puked on your rug trouble? LOL. And what timeframe
are we talking about? Within the last 5 years or since that shared
first gallon jug of Country Roads Apple Wine back in high school? I
opt to check one box up from false. I feel that is fair given the
wide scope the structure of the question allowed! LOL.

The psychologist was in to see me first thing this morning. We speak.
I update her on my concerns and provide her with the "context"
of some of my answers and point out the scribbles I made where I
felt they were required.

She says, "Words are important to you." Out loud I say, "Yes"
inside I am thinking, "oh is this indicative of a personality
type?" I explain that most of these types of test I could respond
with "that depends." The context and my mood will impact my
answer – always.

Anyway, she is very nice and I am happy to hear that she will pop
in tomorrow, and follow up next week. Aside from her comments
that made me wonder if I am being too optimistic (Dan re-assured
me I am being optimistic while still being realistic) I came out
unscathed. LOL!

So we got up at 5:40, fought traffic and arrived at 7:45, 15
minutes late thanks to traffic and snow, all I can tell you is,
I have given blood, handed back my psychology "test" and now at
10:30 I sit here waiting, which is okay – only because writing
this email is a good distraction.

More later,

Carole

January 22, 2008
Re: Too funny!

Hi Guys,

Oh my Gosh! So what started as an innocent, logical question has turned into something very interesting. I have dust allergies that in past years caused me to wake up so stuffed up I couldn't breathe. So when I first got diagnosed, I asked the Oncologist if I could continue my maintenance level dose of allergy shots. MJ, my trusty local nurse agreed to give shots when I got the blessing from the Oncologist. I got my once a month shot during the first two rounds of Chemo. My allergies were under control, chemo proving very effective. Just prior to my 3rd round I got my same allergy shot. Within 20 minutes I developed hives on my hands and stomach. A reaction I had never had in 2 years taking the shots, but a reaction I had in my past due to my dust allergy once, when I was stressed out.

So of course I start to think, my immune system is weakened after 2 rounds of chemo - just like when you are stressed out your immune system is low . . . Now, twice I got hives from dust! I decided not to take any more allergy shots. But this begs the question who is the best person to ask the question "is it okay to continue taking my allergy shots?" Oncologist, GP or Allergist - this time I ask the nurse at the cancer clinic - she agrees to ask the Oncology Pharmacist. Yesterday she called. She didn't have an answer but agreed to look into it. Today we met. After a discussion about my meds for nausea and pain, our conversation turns to allergy medication. She searched her database - there is absolutely nothing on the topic!! Terry/Gwen - it turns out I may be the only cancer patient who ever asked either about OTC allergy meds or allergy shots!

As it stands, I still don't have a definitive answer. However, the pharmacist is doing a presentation on my case next week to the other pharmacists, based on these questions I am asking. Hey maybe there is a histamine cancer therapy in the making!
We then talk about my lack of need for medication - but abundance of vitamins (never above recommended daily values) but again the Milk Thistle supplement the "liver protectorant" raises eyebrows. I will follow up with her on the amount. She writes it down, I am sure she is Googling it as I type. LOL

So maybe I will become the first documented case of chemo and allergy therapy in parallel and set a precedent!

As my chemo "pusher", I decide to ask her about heated IP chemo. Her eyebrows lift as she tells me she just looked at it yesterday, that they currently do not do it, but she hadn't even printed off the article! I tell her about my daily hot baths and nightly hot water bottle on my abdomen routine. She is fine with it. (I brought my hot water bottle!) She is going to look at that one as well! I tell her to call me if she wants to ask me about the heat, the milk thistle or about my allergies! This all bodes well for my proactive approach! My spirits are high! My drugs are here!

Talk to you soon,

Carole

January 22, 2008
Re: Words flowing today

Hi Guys,

I am being somewhat of a pest today, however when the words flow, and creativity flows you have to "respect" it and honor it with your efforts to capture it – so out it comes to all of you!

Once again I am sharing a room. Something that has never been a good experience for me! Upon reflection, over time, it seems hard enough to sleep the whole night through with the man I love and have known for 27 years, let alone a stranger with Lord knows what sleeping habits! Well that's not entirely true, I know my overnight roomy is a big snorer – as she slept and snored most of the day. What will she do tonight!! When she was awake she ate, went out for a smoke and complained about pain. I feel for her and hope that I will not be like that. Her age is a mystery to me. She looks older than me but not much. She looks hard, perhaps from chemo, perhaps from living a hard life. When Dan and I first arrived, she got up to go to the washroom. She forgot to shut the door – I reminded her Dan was in the room. Was this the pain or meds? Did she no longer care? Had she not heard Dan's voice? I think back to one of the psychologist's questions: Do you care about how you look and what other's think? I had responded with "somewhat" – which is typically me! But next to my roommate I guess I should have answered "true". Anyway I am sure I will survive a stranger's snores as well as my loving husband's snoring LOL!

I recall that all my hospital stays in shared rooms have really been difficult for me.

In grade 10 I had my webbed toes separated. (Yes I gave up March break – Mom insisted I not miss school, for such trivial surgery! As it turns out not so trivial . . . I asked Dan – he never would have married me if I still had webbed toes LOL!) Anyway, there was no Children's hospital back then so I was in the Civic in a four, bed ward. They took an elderly lady out on a gurney and despite my Demerol buzz I witnessed this and asked the nurse where they were taking her. She had died. About an hour later they brought her back in! I asked the nurse why they brought her back! The nurse explained she was a different elderly lady. (She looked the same to me . . .) Within a half hour I had been moved to another ward (good heads up on the nurses' part) with young "old ladies" in their 30's! They seemed much less sick and I even befriended a lady from Chapleau whom I corresponded with a few times.

Next time in the hospital I was 21 when I broke my back in a car accident. This time I had coverage for a private room but my Mom, heart in the right place, thought I would like someone to talk to for my 10-day stay. Good theory but not good outcome. I was with an elderly lady who groaned all night. I moved to a private room after one night – and slept well for 9 more nights. For now I have another roomy and she is here to help me develop sympathy.

. . . The cadence of her voice gives her away. She is medicated to the point – you can hear it. It is like being a DD and hearing someone who would blow over .08 . . . but not bad enough to weave over the middle line, just bad enough to weave within the lines and brake just a tad to sporadically. Despite this I am encouraged as she seems lucid enough to ask the doctors and nurses about her medication and tells them about her weekend with her brother. After a couple of phone calls from a friend and someone else whom I could not determine from my circumstantial eavesdropping, she seems happier, wheezing less and I almost denote a tone of optimism in her voice. I feel better now at her circumstance – which is good, because one cannot help but see her, as a potential reflection of me sometime in the future . . .

The nurse walks in to take my blood pressure and heart rate. Gee I am healthy! We chat about advances in chemo since she started her nursing career in oncology in London Ont. years ago. This topic came up since I am receiving an older, stronger chemo called cisplatin, which they are using again since it has been made easier to handle with the new anti - nausea drugs, including one called Emend that only became available in Canada 2 weeks ago! I ask her if she watched Star Trek. Did she see the episode where they travel back to earth to our time and Dr. McCoy is appalled when he sees our surgeons "butchering" - operating on a patient. McCoy waves his 24th century wand over the guy and heals him. We laugh at the possibility . . . but that day will come! If we can think it, we can create it. I think back about Josh and losing his identical twin to "Twin to Twin transfusion" and only 5 years later they have an in utero operation to repair the problem! Again I become optimistic, if I can get rid of it now I can keep it away - if not forever but until they develop something new!

Thanks for "listening" and being my support group.

Carole

January 23, 2008
Subject: Roommate mystery revealed

Hi Guys,

A short one today! My observations of my hospital roommate of yesterday have a new light on them today after a night together! Yesterday she was snoring most of the day. I had prepared myself for a night of snoring - got that one licked with my good headphones. Not so much the solution! It turns out she is a night owl. I woke up at 1:00 am to roll over and my IV came out. The nurses got it sorted out. Then I went for a pee. It was then that I woke up enough to notice my roommate was wide, awake. She was watching TV and her light was on. I settle back in, begin my pseudo meditation/relaxation/incantation . . . by 2pm the smell of my roomies pungent late night snack wafted over to my bed so

I gave up. I asked the nurse for a teeny, tiny sleeping pill. The secret of my roomies ability to sleep all day is answered. She stays up all night! Modern medicine pulsing around my body I sleep well for the rest of the night! Ahhhh sleep is good - energy replenished to fight and recover.

Tomorrow - I'll tell you if I passed my psychology test ha-ha! Just a sneak peek - you guys have been my study partners and are my homework!

Love you all,

Carole

January 23, 2008
Re: You know the joke about the black sheep.

Hi Guys,

My Mom and Dad just left after a visit in the hospital. They mentioned they had read my emails yesterday about the semi private versus private rooms. My mom says "thanks" with a note of sarcasm in her voice! She then adds, "Its like a game of Russian roulette - you can end up with someone who is good company or someone who is bad. In my experience I have had some very nice chats with my hospital roommates . . ."
"Dad," I quickly interjected, "perhaps mom never had bad roommates because she WAS the bad roommate" LOL!! "I'm just teasing Mom . . . but it's like the joke - every family has a black sheep. If you can't see one in your family, you're it!"

Carole

January 23, 2008
Subject: D'Oh

Hi Guys

Just a quick sorry for all the typos in my last mail! (Now edited for the book) Hey I have an IV in one arm, a catheter on top of my rib cage under my skin that is now delivering chemo laced alcohol into my system, I just finished a 24 hour long chemo/alcohol fest that started with Benadryl and was chased with a 2pm sleeping pill. I figure that, along with using my blackberry keyboard with my stubby fingers, gives me a good excuse ;-)

Carole

January 25, 2008
Re: The Joke about the bear in the woods

Hi Guys,

So there's the joke about running away from a bear . . . you don't have to be the fastest runner, you just have to be ahead of one guy! This joke came to my head in the hospital the other day when I was talking to the psychotherapist. She said that I have some very good tools, in my "defense mechanism pool" I use intellect and humor, which as she says, at the other end of the scale is curling up in a corner sucking on my thumb and rocking so I am at the good end of the scale. She did warn me about letting the emotions out and not always being too "strong and tough" . . . humm a little to close for comfort :-) I did explain to her that over the last 4 months I have cried more than I have in my entire adult life! I have been letting out emotions in these writings to all of you and that many of you sent me back emails writing . . . "gee I didn't know that about you", or "I didn't think you were that funny", so, I think this whole experience is allowing me to open up. So I did tell her about all of you guys, who are helping along the way. Anyway back to the joke. In this conversation with the psychotherapist it occurred to me. I have been breaking this down into smaller bite size pieces (yes my project management skills are coming into play) I had determined that step 1/ get rid of this cancer. 2/ Change my lifestyle as much as I can to help so it won't come back 3/ Live a long, long life. I have a lot more to do but step 3 was too big . . . this is what was causing my fears. Until this week! I realize I don't have to look at step 3 as big and as daunting as I have been. All I need to do is run faster than one guy . . . if I can stay in remission until the next big breakthrough then I am good to go.

I don't know. To me this seems like a logical approach. I have a plan - ahhhh. I have "emoted" to all of you - ahhhh - I will tell "my therapist". All is well.

Carole

January 25, 2008
Subject: RE: The joke about the bear in the
**   woods . . . .**

OK tears in the office, is just bad form . . . cellmate ran over
to see if I was ok . . . LOL!
Quick Kleenex and a laugh . . . Just fine I say . . . Just got a
really nice email from a really nice friend!

Sonya

January 25, 2008
Subject: RE: The joke about the bear in the
**   woods . . .**

Thanks a lot Sonya! I was fine until I got your reply . . . Now
I'm the one looking for Kleenex!

Thanks for sharing your thoughts with us Carole. And all my bets
are on you out-running whomever, whatever, whenever, wherever.
Hell, you'll probably come up with the cure yourself! Hope those
researchers are prepared to listen and take notes!!

Cathy

January 29, 2008
Subject: Me on a leash

Hi Guys,

With this IP chemo treatment, I now have two visits to the hospital
in a cycle. Last week was the overnight stay. Today is a day only
treatment.

I forgot to tell you about my overnight stay last week. Here is
what my IP chemo treatment was all about . . .

First I got a Pic/PIC? line inserted in me . . . this is something
that is new to me. This pic line goes in my upper forearm. It
will deliver my 'regular' chemo, Benadryl, fluids for hydration,
red wine . . . or whatever they decide.

They numbed my skin, then they stuck a wire-guided tube into my vein, which they found via a portable ultrasound machine. This is all good – except for one thing . . . . the nurse and her "student" were conversing about how to do this procedure. Then the nurse said "Mrs. McCaskill can you turn your chin and tuck it into the shoulder" (on the side where they are sticking the pic line) and she demonstrated. "No problem," I said. Then they started talking French to each other. My French is quite rudimentary so to me it sounded kinda like the Charlie Brown teacher wah, wah, wah JUGULAR, wah, wah. "Okay what was the Jugular comment?" "Oh this vein could go up towards my jugular – my head movement protects the pic line from going up to my jugular and makes it go down my arm." Oh comforting – but they brought in a portable X-Ray to make sure that it is going in the right direction.

Oh, I also found out that my veins are tough . . . this is good because chemo makes the veins collapse – this will help I am sure . . .

So moving from the pic in my arm to the catheter (you know the one that feels like I have something in my breast pocket jabbing me – but I can't remove it) sitting on top of my ribs. Now it's the time to insert a needle into this catheter. Let me tell you, I have no fear of needles but somehow this one is pretty scary. It is about 1.5 inches long and awfully thick and was about to be stuck into my ribs, as Dan reminded me, akin to the scene from Pulp Fiction where they injected the needle directly into the heart . . . not quite as scary, but close! It took 3 tries to get it in the right spot. (I did try to control myself on the swearing as this was occurring . . . my mom and dad were sitting at the foot of my bed – okay – no English swear words. I am in a bilingual hospital – no French swear words. So now I revert to my pseudo French swear words . . . mon dit, colin de bin, taberwit – Shit! That wasn't too bad considering the size of that needle they were stabbing into me!!) It is not such a science as an art I guess. Three nurses but we did it. After all of that, the actual IP Chemo is somewhat of a let down! After everything is in me, they invert me in my bed so that all this chemo reaches the top part of my abdomen. My yoga training will come into effect – I did a bridge pose – kind of an inverted, resting on my shoulders pose with my belly up in the air. If that didn't help, I think the pot holed road situation in Ottawa, which was the scorn of my trip home after surgery, was an additional "shake 'n bake" to stir up this chemo so it hits every nook and cranny!

So the pic line was bad enough – but when they use it to attach you to the pump and IV giving you fluids – it is like a leash! I understand it's required to ensure all goes well with the chemo but my leash is a constant reminder that I am "sick". For the most part I can go about my day to day business without the pulsing tone of a 9 volt battery pump, pushing a one liter bag of saline solution into my system via a "pic line" that for all I know "could have been inadvertently pumping fluids into my jugular" . . . well you know something risky like that . . . LOL.

After a full 24 hours of hydration pumped into me, the home nurse removed the pump from my pic line. I hated it – I am happy that it helped me get through this "tougher" than the last round unscathed.

Now back to today. I received my next round of chemo delivered via my newly inserted PIC line last week. This was a quick visit, no nausea pills to take, no hydration and other than 3 inches back on my waistline (feels like bloating.) This is an easy day. The nurses saw me walk in, ordered my chemo before even checking my blood! They are quite amazed how little impact this round has affected me. They do take blood anyway. For those who like numbers, here's the count. As a reminder – a normal CA125 blood test is 0-35. When I came in I was 3335. After one round of chemo, – 935! It was 46 after 2 rounds of chemo, after surgery I was 9, today it is 8! This is fabulous. Of course I want a zero. Dan hopped on this and asked the nurse who said she has never seen it 0 or 1. (Wouldn't it be nice if everyone got one test at age 40 to get a personal baseline CA 125 report.) . . . Back on track . . . Perhaps less sugar in my diet maybe I can prove something and get a 0 ;-) The nurse did say my magnesium was a tiny bit low. They gave me some intravenously last week with the IP chemo. This treatment apparently depletes magnesium. I take a supplement once a day. I did forget yesterday . . . I ask the nurse how much I needed. She said I should take two a day – now this is what I am talking about! I can do this to help myself.

Of course I would not be sad if it stays at 8 since it is low in the normal range in the general population. However . . . I have a target. Of course I also want a hole in one – if I never get one it doesn't take away from birdies and pars and it sounds like I am hitting par for the course right now. (By the way . . . you have put up with my ramblings to the tune of about 30,000 words – and surprisingly this is my first golf reference!)

I look around the chemo room and I am the only one who is not "jaundiced" yellow. The young 25-year-old Christine, that I met my first day in chemo is in today as well. This is her last treatment. She is sallow . . . but her spirits seem high. She needs blood though in order for her chemo to happen today. She is not receiving IP Chemo – only through IV. I feel guilty – I am sure she is looking at me, and wonders why I am taking it so well. I certainly look the healthiest in this room – I know, I know – the best of the worse . . . not really that great an accolade. We exchange stories about hot flashes. She can recall her having one or two of them. I have about 3 a day! I would rather be sweating – then some of the other problems that some patients in here have. When I left today, as I walked out, I said to her with a smile "I hope I never see you again". It is her last trip here and I am sure she is happy. Her mom had a broad smile.

Oh by the way – this cancer is like an up and down yoyo diet. After the IP chemo, I added about 6 or 7 lbs and about 3 inches to my waist – overnight! It has dissipated (read absorbed into my body) and out through my septic tank in about 3 days. Considering I left the hospital with a red bag for "biohazards" in case I did get nauseous and needed to return it to the hospital, that begs the question – how much chemo can my septic system take? I wonder if anyone has thought about all of this . . . hmmm another Google search for another day! Perhaps we have found the root cause of male pattern baldness LOL . . . or more probable – perhaps this is some of the trouble frogs are experiencing.

February 4, 2008
Subject: Carpe Diem

Hi Guys,

At coffee club this morning we were discussing missed opportunities. When I reflect back on the things that are "missed opportunities", they all have to do with travel. When I was in Miami on business the person I was with didn't want to go to a Miami Dolphin's game. That's one. When I was in Washington DC on business the person I was travelling with, didn't want to go to the US Open. I didn't go. That's two. When I was in San Francisco I missed the drive along the A1A Coastal highway because the guy I was travelling with thought he could drive in a strange city and read a map at the same time, better than me reading the map, and despite my pleas to give me the map . . . thought he could do better. That one stung – that was three. Then I took a trip to Phoenix on business. My parents had told me about this 'road trip' they had taken previously. Three of us cancelled our flights to Las Vegas, rented a car and drove the back roads from Phoenix through, Gerome, Sedona, Grand Canyon, Hoover Dam and on to Vegas. That was the most spectacular trip. Last year, Dan, Josh and my mother in law took the trip. Again spectacular! With the weather today so warm I think about – 74 more sleeps until my "Spring Opener" golf tournament, only two more chemo sessions, and a shopping trip yesterday to buy smaller size pants for "back to work" this summer!" My thoughts turn to a summer vacation trip . . . it is not a matter of if – it is only a matter of where to go! We are thinking of a riverboat cruise along the Danube from Budapest with a side trip to Prague! But hey, maybe we'll wait a bit and head down east, out west or north . . .

I am shifting my thoughts from "cancer patient" to "cancer survivor" . . . with this new title comes a renewed validation of my philosophy . . . carpe Diem . . . seize the day. My Great Aunt "Mu" said to me when I was in my 20's, "Don't wait to travel and do the things you want until you are retired. You may get sick and may not be able to enjoy all the money you saved for retirement and won't be able to travel". It is also tax time . . . so I guess it is all about balance . . . RRSPs but save some money for a really nice vacation.

Reflections this morning have probably been brought on to our loss of a coffee club member. Doug died on the weekend. He was 84. He had a full wonderful life. He brought many interesting stories to the coffee club. He made his way to The Habour Store, the "host" of our coffee club, right up until 2 weeks ago. We will miss you Doug.

February 6, 2008
Subject: Inspiration and Humility

Hi Guys,

There is a poem that I keep reading on those endless emails about
friends coming into and out of your life and that there is always
some meaning to these 'encounters.' This journey has been filled
with serendipity, coincidence, fate or whatever you may call it.
There is one that trumps all others. In mid September, when the
weather was just starting to change, and the conversation around
the coffee club picnic table turned to discussions on how many
more days we would be able to "conduct our business" outside
the store at the picnic table before the weather forced us to
our table inside. As typical with the coffee club, a stranger
is always welcomed with a "hello", and if the timing was right
and a quick and friendly response back was received, we offered
back "would you like to take the quiz?" Or perhaps "what brings
you to the Harbour?" or "where are you from?" That mid September
morning, she walked up. Her hair was cropped short, short enough
to stand straight up without any mousse to hold it up. The sides
were brushed back. A T-shirt, jeans, big black boots and a belt
buckle with, what looked like, from a quick sideways glance, and
later confirmed, DaVinci's Last Supper. Her voice was low, calm
and had a melodic lilt. I think she was asking where to find a gas
station . . . honestly I didn't pay much attention, or perhaps my
first coffee of the day hadn't kicked in yet. Her name was Ivan.
She was camping in the park. Although our concern over the change
in weather was going to move us indoors for coffee, Ivan's concern
about the weather was over finding a place to stay for the winter as
her trailer was already starting to get cold at night. When Ivan
showed up the next morning we learned that she was a published
author, was the "Author in Residence" at Carleton University and
was going to be in town for while. Ivan came to coffee club all
that week. On the Friday, I bought her book Bow Grip, out of the
back of her truck. I wanted to support her. I wanted an autographed
copy. It would be great in my book collection. But mostly I was
in awe. I had always wanted to write." Perhaps I could take your
night course." "You should start by journaling"

I read her book on my way down to Phoenix on business. What a
wonderful read. The next time I saw Ivan, I had just been told I

had cancer. When we spoke, I told her that she had come into my life for a reason. The next week, she asked me if I had started writing. I had not. Ivan lent me her digital micro tape recorder. Then I started writing my emails to all of you – in earnest. With all of you suggesting that I write a book. My decision was to turn my emails into a book. I also began writing my thoughts and began to sort out my feelings. By the time it got to November, "Novel Writing Month" I was in full swing thanks to Ivan's suggestion to join the contest. If you have seen me lately you will see that I wear a black baseball cap that reads "Writers Aloud." Ivan gave me that hat from one of her storytelling gigs. I wear the hat every morning to coffee club. It is my daily inspiration to keep writing. I am at 35,000 words. I have two more chemo sessions, surgery to remove my catheter, removal of my PIC line, about 10 more topics I haven't written yet but logged in my blackberry so as not to forget them and apparently 3 months to "recover" before I head back to work. Certainly enough time and inspiration to write about 15,000 more words (Ivan says I need at least 50,000) and following Ivan's advice – "write now – edit later" – I will need a few more months to edit. Perhaps that is during my "recovery time."

In October I went to see Ivan perform. Her voice is like an instrument. It is melodic. It soothes you, painting a vivid picture on every carefully chosen word. It draws you closer to the climax so subtly at times that each word turns the corners of your mouth up into a grin when she sweeps you up with a laugh that speaks the truth and fills your heart. If her voice is the melody, her words are the music. There are only so many musical notes and there are only so many words . . . it is how you string them together that makes the difference. It is now that I understand why we can use the word composition for both music and writing. I listened to a new story that Ivan had just written. It is about the coffee club. When hearing this story where Ivan describes people I know it all became very clear to me what it is that makes Ivan's writing, "composing." She teases us with her words. They are carefully chosen words . . . somehow they leave you wanting more, but somehow leaving you satisfied.

It was Ivan who pointed out that we met when I first got diagnosed and that her contract with the University ends a week after my April 15th "end of treatment" appointment. Did Ivan come into my life

for a reason? I think so. I am truly inspired and humbled. If you
are on this list and live in Ottawa and want to hear Ivan perform,
come to the winter carnival in Fitzroy Harbour at 8pm this Friday.
If you are out of town, buy Bow Grip, visit www.ivanecoyote.com
or buy one of her other 3 books, you will enjoy them. Perhaps I
can begin to repay the support and inspiration . . .

Carole

February 7, 2008
Subject: Perhaps a comb over . . .

Hi Guys,

If you haven't seen me lately, my hair is starting to come back. (I will lose it again – probably with this next round of chemo) So I noticed that my hair started coming back after about 4 weeks without chemo in my system. Even after one round of chemo after my surgery, my hair growth is about 8 weeks "long". My hair is actually longer than some of my "follically-challenged" male friends and Dan. So I think it is about a 1 on the shaver.

As I begin to think about the end of my treatment, I have started to prepare to go back to the "real world" Here are some pluses:

1. I have bought some new pants, as my old ones are too big. In the end my weight is much healthier now.
2. I have a greater appreciation for root vegetables. They are part of my eating habits from now on.
3. I have eliminated many processed foods and have grown in my love of cooking (I made a killer soup last Saturday from scratch – instead of pulling out a can or packaged soup)
4. Thanks to my belly button down scar I have eliminated a few tops and bottoms that at 46 I was probably too old to wear anyway!
5. I love gardening – and now my garden will be even bigger with vegetables in it.
6. After so many years with long hair, I really have grown to love my hair short. Remember my pre bald hair cut that I loved and thought I would adopt – I'm thinking it might even be shorter. I mean real short.

This morning at coffee, I was discussing my hair and how I now realize why my hair was always a pain to "control." With it so short I can see that one side of my hair lies flat on my head and tends toward the back of my head . . . as one would expect. The other side has one 5 inch triangle where the hair goes against the grain and points towards my face! On top of my head is a swirl – which I assume is my cowlick coming back. Then there is some weird ridge that I can't see very well at the back of my head that seems to stand at attention – away from my head. As we discussed this, Gwen mentioned that my "triangle hair wedge" looked like the beginning of a comb over . . . hummm that is something to consider. I've never seen a woman with a comb over. I guess there must be someone, somewhere . . . hummm . . . maybe . . . a Mohawk . . . when you're starting from scratch . . . a new beginning – there are endless possibilities . . . life is looking good on the other side of this journey!

Carole

February 12, 2008
Re: My Husband is in love with a lesbian clown!

Hi Guys,

I am sitting in bed in the hospital for my treatments to start and waiting for inspiration or something funny to happen to write to you, my "Hi Guys" as I have come to call it.

This time I got my private room so I was sitting in my bed thinking that I was going to get a much better night sleep than the last time I was in! However Dan is sick today so he is going to go home in a while. My TV is not hooked up yet but I brought a book, have the paper and of course my blackberry. Oh, don't worry, I'll explain the "subject line" of this email, but it will wait ;-)

So here I am in my room about to compose my email entitled mea culpa. Saying that my Mom may have been right about having a roommate since it is so quiet in here and no TV to create background noise. Well ask for it and it will be delivered. My neighbor in the next room, separated by walls . . . woke up and he is old and hard of hearing. How do I know this? His TV is blasting out Regis and skinny lady?? Now I am hoping he will watch Rachel Ray and The View – my normal background "noise." I also hope he goes to bed early or we may have dueling TVs tonight! I just got up and checked. With the door closed it is still loud. The doctor just yelled how good he looks and is improving (in case you were curious) and the Doctor said he would look for his glasses that he thought he left downstairs in Module K! It is all I can do to stop myself from asking the doctor to look for his hearing aid at the same time.

Although the PICC (I believe is the correct acronym) in my arm
is a pain I am happy this morning when they drew blood and they
left my veins alone!

Okay, so if you've been following along, you know that Ivan
performed at the Fitzroy Winter Carnival. I'm not sure if I've
mentioned it but also performing with her was Mooky. Mooky is an
ex Cirque du Soleil clown, a friend of Ivan's, who wandered into
town. She was absolutely gut splitting hilarious! Ivan brought
her to coffee club a while back where the idea was hatched for
this performance by the two of them. Mooky has shoulder length
dirty blonde dreadlocks. When asked where she lives, she responds
"out of my shoes". This clown is fairly low key – which we learn
later – she is probably a type B minus! Nothing seems to faze
her. We "booked" the show, she left and turned up last week. The
morning of the show, she seemed so calm, yet seemingly unprepared,
at least by my Type A personality standards. You know me I had
two back up plans in case the wireless MIC ran out of batteries!
Mooky was slowly setting up her stage while chatting on the
phone. Her life is in two jumbo size Rubbermaid containers and
a 4 drawer plastic container on wheels, taped down to hold the
drawers shut for transport. Her background music (and later I
learned, an integral part of her act) is on an iPod. This is where
it all begins . . .

Dan was the audio man for the show. After several dress rehearsals
to prepare for one especially time sensitive music queue, and
several purposeful missed queues by Dan, trying to see if Mooky's
calm exterior, could be broken, Dan was intrigued . . . Prior to
the performance we had one Mooky emergency (she needed scissors to
trim her hair so it would not show with her wig on) not bad for
zero back up plans! (Perhaps there is something to Mooky's Zen like
calm) Mooky transformed to Gloria, a blonde wigged, overdone blue
eye shadowed, bright red lipsticked clown in a peach coloured tutu
with granny underpants hanging out from under the ruffles. If that
wasn't funny enough, as one person in the audience quipped, "she
hasn't even talked yet and I'm just laughing at her expressions!"
Mooky was a wonderful surprise and Ivan captivated the audience, as I
knew she would, but this story is about Dan and the clown . . .
After the performance we invited Ivan and Mooky back to our place
to watch a DVD of Pink Floyd and have beer or something. We all
chatted a bit, listened to Pink Floyd and The Last Waltz by The

Band. Ivan even commented how much Dan and Mooky are so much alike. Dan a clown – okay. Dan type B minus, Zen like creature – not so much! Maybe I see him differently. The next morning at coffee Dan grilled Mooky about her philosophy and many other questions. When we got home I said to Dan "you looove Mooky!" He said, "I do." Aside from Mooky's sexual orientation making this funny and an obvious unrequited love situation evolving . . . is, as many of you know, is even funnier since Dan has always been petrified of clowns! I mean "you can't be serious" petrified! Perhaps Mooky has started getting him over his phobia of clowns.

What a great winter carnival weekend. It was nice to forget about things, stay out late and see loads of friends! Our 11th annual McCaskill Trivia was fun as always. It was great to see many of you in person this weekend.

Martha Stewart is blasting from the TV next door – I see a bad moon on the rise!

Funny, just as I typed this, the GP Oncologist walked in and said my white count was .1 below where it needs to be so I have to go home and come back next week. This has nothing to do with the cancer going up, only that the chemo impacting my white count. I asked – it has nothing to do with eating or not getting enough rest over the winter carnival weekend or anything like that. Delay until Monday at least. I am not happy. There is a drug I can take. Apparently it will help my white count that I can take after the next treatment. There is nothing that can be done for today. Another search on the Internet this afternoon – maybe I can find something I can do to help bring my white count back up.

Next week!

Carole

February 12, 2008
Subject: Back home . . . to grow more blood cells.

Hi Guys,

I am back home after a "missed" chemo session due to my low white cell count. There is a $2000 drug the hospital said I could take for the next treatment. (Which is not be covered by OHIP nor by my drug plan) I asked about eating healthy or what can I do to help. I was told "nothing really". I Googled it! Zinc helps white blood cell production. Apparently yogurt, nuts, beans, and red meat are high in Zinc . . . as I gobbled down my second helping of yogurt!
I go back next week. One extra week! Let's hold it at that, and get 'er done!

See you soon,

Carole

February 14, 2008
Subject: Happy Valentines Day

Hi Guys,

Happy Valentines Day!

Today I will "introduce everyone to everyone" I want this in the book so I will not use last names. This is the list of my "Hi Guys" email list. There are so many other friends, family and co-workers that are very near and special to me and are not on my Hi Guys list so please remember I love all of you and the support you give me.

The two people not on this list are by far the most important. First is Dan, who is the love of my life, my soul mate, and all those other clichés. I cannot imagine life without him and I cannot imagine going through this journey without his absolute devotion, support and commitment to making this as easy as it can be. He often says he feels helpless in helping me and has no control over making me better. Many of you have said how strong and positive I am. Without Dan my strength is gone. He is my best friend. C.S. Lewis said "Friendship is unnecessary . . . It has no survival value; rather it is one of those things which give value to survival." Josh, my wonderful son, who like any mom, I could go on and on about how wonderful he is – so I won't. I will say that Dan and I took 6 years to get pregnant where others seem to take months. We lost his identical twin. He was born at 6 months gestation. Every single day with Josh is a miracle, we treasure. We are constantly surprised by the wonderful personality we see unfolding in Josh. There is so much more to learn about him and his story that is unfolding. This is what gives me strength and a positive attitude.

All of you have touched my life in the past and now in this journey that I unwillingly take. You provide me with a sounding board. You are my support group and my inspiration. Thanks to all of you for "lending me your ears". You have all helped me out from food, to gifts, to caroling, to driving me around, adapting menus to meet my weird cancer diet, sending me tidbits you found on the internet, jokes of the day, a phone call or email – just to say you are thinking of me. You have all helped me.

Carole

Go to the back of the book to read about the wonderful people included in my living journal and read a funny story about them!

February 18, 2008
Subject: Thanks

For those who are reading this (assuming this becomes a book!) that I count among my circle of friends and family that are not on my "Hi Guys" emails, I wanted to give you the nod of thanks and support. Many of you, whom I talked to daily, kept me company and phoned to find out my status! Thanks to my father in law, Graham, my brothers in law, Lee and Lorne, my brother, Pat and Denise, and all my nieces and nephews and cousins. The husbands of my friends whom are always there, Brian, Ken, Rob, Rick and Rick, Gord, Ben, Terry, John and the rest of the men in our social circle! Also our local coffee club members: Vace, Pete, Linda, Clayton, Debbie, Dave, Faye, Lorne, Bert, Tina, Jim and Norma.

Carole

February 18, 2008
Subject: Wrinkle Free goes Green

Hi Guys,

In many of these emails I have been telling you about chemicals (parabens, SLS and others) that are "suspect", when it comes to cancer. Consequently I have eliminated most of these from my life. At the same time, especially after my hysterectomy, I have been worrying about wrinkles and other signs of aging . . . since I got rid of all my very expensive wrinkle creams. Over the weekend, surfing on-line, I found some natural substitutes for cosmetics.

Wrinkle Wrangler

4 drops hazelnut oil
2 teaspoon almond oil
9 drops sweet orange essential oil

Combine, massage into the skin morning and night.

Tired Skin Green Tea Tonic

Steep green tea, cool, apply . . . use daily for best results

Face Mask Salad!

1/2 C heavy cream
1 carrot cooked and mashed
1 Avocado, peeled, pitted and mashed
3 T of honey

Combine ingredients, spread over face for 12 minutes, and rinse
with cool water
Improves skins texture, diminish age spots and rebuilds skin
collagen when used with regularity.

Pina Colada Cream for Dry Skin

1 egg
1/4 C sesame oil
1/4 C sunflower oil
1 T liquid lecithin
1 T fresh lemon juice
1/2 C Coconut oil

Blend all ingredients on low, until mixture is thick. Refrigerate
for one hour, blend again on low. Apply to face before bed.
(Don't drink!!!!!!)

The Lecithin helps rebuild and regenerate cell tissue. Coconut
oil helps seal in the skins moisture.

Okay so I haven't tried any of these. But I'm going to. In the
meantime I have found many products both at the health food store
but also in the regular Pharmacy. They are out there and are not too
expensive. For anyone with teenagers and want a cheap, safe blemish
cream, Burt's Bees have a product, but also, good old fashioned witch
hazel with a few drops of Tea tree oil (at the pharmacy) applied
as an astringent works well without the chemicals. Even Wal-Mart
is carrying green (paraben and SLS free) shampoo and conditioner!

I am back into my overnight Chemo treatment tomorrow . . . so be forewarned . . . if I send an email . . . it will be drug and alcohol induced, done on my blackberry which is next to impossible to edit . . . especially drugged up.

Carole

February 19, 2008
Re: Starting off bad

Hi Guys,

It was dark driving down the Carp Road at 6am this morning. The wind was blowing hard and the snow has hit again, causing seeming endless delays on the 417. Thus explaining the dent in our dash where my boot had been pressed against it, in an effort to help Dan with the breaks. Multiple swear words cursing the traffic, roads and winter in general, capped off with a one finger salute to the cop stopped on the side of the road causing even more delays, made up our two hour trip to the hospital.

Dan dropped me off and I rush to admitting. I only rush because I have to go to the bathroom, of course. The printer in admitting broke down, what are another few minutes after an hour wait? I think this is good training for my bladder for our next long road trip.

Here's where it gets bad or good depending how you look at it. Remember my trials the last time when sharing a room? Now I am in a ward. That means 3 other people. So sleep will be interesting . . . but hey there should be plenty of interesting tales to tell.

In fact one story has already begun to unfold as I type this. One lady is moaning. You know, really moaning. It is reminiscent of the moaning Billy Crystal did in "When Harry Met Sally" when he was really depressed. Moaning constantly – even after the nurse gave her a pill and told her to press her morphine pump to help her after her hip surgery for a broken hip. I feel sorry but ohhhhh.

. . . Now it is quiet, except for the snoring of roommate number 2. The hip lady just got herself out of bed, into a wheelchair and out. Where would she be going? Is she supposed to be up after hip surgery? She didn't have a coat on. If she is going outside she will not be happy. Perhaps her pill has kicked in and when she gets back she will have stopped moaning.

Now Dan and I will disturb them . . . he is back with Timmy's and the paper. As with every morning, it is time for the Sun newspaper quiz.

I am sure I will email again soon ;-)

Carole

February 19, 2008
Re: Now we've done it!

Hi Guys,

We woke up roommate number 2 while doing the quiz . . . at least I think so, her eyes are half open and she is staring at me. She does not have cancer so I guess I am an oddity to her. She is very old so I won't yell at her to stop staring!!! LOL . . . correction laughing in my head! However I may erupt soon at the Moaner. She came back from her "stroll", told the nurse to turn off our shared overhead lights because roommate 3 doesn't like them. (I am thinking she could shut the blinds, since she has the window, and keep the lights on so I can see to keep writing this to you guys!!!) Then the "Moaner" gets up and leaves and tells Dan to turn on the lights???

To top things off I checked out the washroom that the 4 of us share and I am not a clean freak but somebody left their toothbrush and stuff on the little shelf beside a urine specimen bottle - with the seal "cracked". I'm not sure if it had urine in it or if someone thought it would be good to use to transport her toothbrush in!

Now the" light adverse" roommate, previously known as roommate three, is complaining she wants her chair back, which was in the "common" area of the room, which Dan is using. The "Moaner" tells her there are other chairs. Nobody is happy in this room.

On the up side, my nurse, as always, is nice. The intern, who just started his oncology rotation, is trying to see if he can find a way to help me pay for my $2000 drug. We are still waiting both for an okay that my white count is high enough and also for a semi or private room. (My 3 roommates thank you for letting me vent to you, instead of taking it out on them ;-)

Carole

PS . . . Well, she asked for her chair back. She has her chair.

Benadryl and Blackberry Alert

February 19, 2008
Subject: As much as I joke . . .

Hi Guys,

As much as I joke about my roommates, I feel for them.
The roommate, who hates the light, thought it was Feb 12th. When she found out it was the 19th, she exclaimed how she didn't realize how long she had been in! The moaner found out she has terminal breast cancer that is now in her bones and only found out she had cancer when she broke her hip after 3 months walking on it with just crutches. The last is going home, but she is crying because she is worried about when she can go - her son in law, who looks about 60 and is a volunteer at the hospital is trying to sort out transportation and bringing her a jacket since she came in by ambulance. Again I am thankful. I feel like a dutch out of water in this room. I feel good. The Benadryl is making me dozy and my biggest concern for today is when they will hook up my T.V. And if I switch rooms, will my TV get hooked up in the new room? This day may have started out bad but it has turned out great . . . its all a matter of perspective!

Carole

To: Carole McCaskill
CC: Hi Guys
Subject: RE: As much as I joke . . .

Just wondering . . . If you feel good . . . then would you not
feel like a duck IN water, instead of out of water? Things that
make you go hmmmmm. Then again that benedryl is probably working
just fine . . . . ;) ;)

Cathy

February 19, 2008
Subject: Correction???

. . . . I was thinking that I am a duck out of water, not in, because
I feel emotionally and physically way better than my roommates
so I am "different to them" humm . . .

Carole

To: Carole
CC: Hi Guys
Subject: RE: As much as I joke . . .

Hi Carole,

Are you sure of that? I would say you are feeling a bit 'Dutch'
today . . . hope you have your wooden clogs on . . . I always
feel when I dance a little it is very energizing . . . it may
also cheer up your roomies . . .

Debbie

February 19, 2008
Subject: Re: RE: As much as I joke . . .

Hi Debbie,

I've seen you clog dance! I think it could cheer the room up! I will try to live up to your joyous lead!

Carole

To: Carole
CC: Hi Guys
Subject: RE: As much as I joke . . .

Did you mean Dutch out of water???? :0)

Annette

To: Annette
CC: Hi Guys,
Subject: Re: Re: As much as I joke . . .

LOL how about a dutch out of solder (to mend the dykes they're metal aren't they? ;-) if he had no solder, to repair the dyke that would bring us back to a dutch IN water!

Carole

February 19, 2008
Subject: Arrggghhhhh!

Hi Guys,

The lady who was going home today stayed here – mostly because her son in law scared her when he said they wanted to get her home safely! Now it is 6:45pm and she wants the light out that we all share so she can go to sleep. The "Moaner", whom I suspect is a morphine addict, has been whining for more drugs "the drugs in the needle" she requested, "I'm in so much pain" but seemed okay to go out for her smoke. Then she explained to her nurse that it isn't an addiction – to me this is a clue that it is. However, not my business! Except, she yelled at the nurse to pinch the skin harder! Very mean and also seems like a clue . . . pinch the skin? I would never have thought of that. Anyway, here's the rub. Placated by her hit, she tells the nurse she is removing her patch to go for a smoke . . . and before she leaves, she pipes up to "go ahead and turn out the lights." Me, and the lady whose chair Dan "stole," voted to keep the lights on. The lights are now off. Somehow I find it hard to feel sorry for this lady (the Moaner) I know she is sad and scared but she is just so snarky to all the nurses and the poor clerk answering her "bell" calls. All I want to do is yell out to her "you catch more bees with honey than vinegar" . . . and by the way the bees will be more helpful when you are pleasant . . . after all they are only human! (Well you know what I mean!)

The lights are now off. The moaner has been out of the dark room smoking for 20 minutes, one is watching a small 5-inch TV in the dark, one is asleep and I turn to find solace in my email and have been deep yoga breathing. I have a feeling I will sleep WELL! Against what I like, to sleep without a sleeping pill, I have already asked for one tonight.
Sleep tight!

Carole

February 20, 2008
Re: Ooowatanite

Hi Guys,

Yes 6am is early for me to be emailing you. Of course there's a reason. So glad you asked!

Apparently 2 hits of whatever is in the needle they gave the "Moaner" hit hard and fast and it wears off at 6 in the morning. Her light is on and she's ringing the nurse, asking for more. The nurse said no to the "good" drugs but offered Gravol. She fell asleep in 5 minutes and back to snoring. I am awake.

However, last night was good. No sleeping pill either, despite the snoring, lights and no "The Daily Show with Jon Stewart" lulling me to sleep. How did I do it? Glad you asked! Imagine if you will, a woman in jogging shorts and tank top, required to sleep in that getup, due to 2 drip bags attached to a pump and the night dress didn't work last round . . . all of this to accommodate my "power surges." (My cousin's Linda's term!) Anyway I'm all attached to hoses, in jogging wear, and a once again, very baldhead AND, in an attempt to aid muffling the snoring, I stuffed tampons in my ears! What the heck I don't need them. (Sonya suggested those orange squishy things but I didn't have any. Note to self add orange squishy things for next round.) All was fine with my makeshift ear plugs, hidden behind my dome of silence aka yellow curtain with mesh top; until I went to go to the kitchenette to get a glass of water . . . do I leave the tampons in my ears . . .
No I didn't but really! Like pulling out my already falling out hair at an idiot driver, that would have been a once in a life time opportunity that one could only get away with (pre onset of dementia I guess) when you can say "Hey I have cancer and . . . ?"

Have a great day guys!

Carole

February 20, 2008
Re: Just a short one

Hi Guys,

This morning the lady who couldn't go home, I found out her name
is Della. We started talking. As I suspected her tears yesterday
were because her ex son in law (and his wife - not her daughter)
upset her. I made her a tea - what else is there to do at 7am in
a hospital. So we had our own coffee club! She said to her nurse,
pointing at me, "we're friends now". When you are in a hospital,
in your 80's, concerned about getting your purse and coat back
from where ever it was left when the ambulance brought you in
and worrying how you are getting back to your seniors villa, I
guess a cup of tea and 5 minutes makes a friend. She is sweet and
apparently confused from what I have overheard. But 5 minutes ago
I heard first hand how confused she is. (DON'T LAUGH!) She just
called Dan my son!!! Oh well she is sweet.

Carole

February 20, 2008
Re: Kismet

Hi Guys,

I know you have been inundated with mails but I have to go with
the flow.

My new friend Della and I took a walk. I lent her my slippers, as
she has nothing here with her. I used the hospital blue slippers,
since she felt she would slip. When we got back from our walk she
was hot. Now wouldn't you know it, I had packed a brand new clean
nightdress that I picked up at Winners. It was inexpensive - not
my style, peach flowers, much to warm for hot flashes at home but
covered me better for late night strolls to the bathroom "in
public." I couldn't wear it so I gave it to her since she was
stuck wearing a hospital gown. She put it on, wanted my address
to return it to me. She then offered money, which I refused. I
explained I would never wear it and that last night I was thinking

it was a waste of money. So I guess it was meant to be, to be in a ward and give her my nightdress, a little dignity, and probably most important someone to talk to. Today is a good day.

Carole

February 20, 2008
Subject: "confused about the concept"

Hi Guys,

Well, the "Moaner" continues to flabbergast! She received her first round of chemo today. After they explained everything to her and hooked her up, she began poking at the dangling bag of chemo with her walking stick. Dan and I watched in trepidation. What is she doing? The bag of noxious chemicals fell to the floor. Luckily for her the needle didn't rip out of her arm. Luckily for Della (in the bed next to her) the bag didn't explode when it hit the ground. She looked over expecting Dan to come pick it up for her. We quickly pointed out how the nurses wear real rubber gloves (not latex) and masks and special gowns when handling the chemo and that she should call for a nurse to pick it up. Five minutes after the nurse put it back onto the pole, she started poking at it again, stating she doesn't think it is dripping. We tell her about the lady who got a small splash on her quilt and it burned a hole in the quilt. She stopped poking.

The 'Moaner' has a daughter. She came in for a visit. She is in her twenties. She was discussing how she had missed her exam (when she brought her mom in) and that the school would not let her write it without a doctor's note. The poor daughter could not find a doctor who would write her a note since the mom was sick not the daughter . . . . I feel very sorry for her . . . what a predicament. It seems this is a glimpse at the type of life the daughter has lead . . .

Carole

Benadryl/Blackberry Alert

February 21, 2008
Re: My "virgin" nurse

Hi Guys,

As always, my experience at chemo has been worthy of words! Either
that or I have found a new "Saturday night" relaxer . . . BYOB
now means Bring Your Own Benadryl (on Tap . . . er . . . as an
IV drip I mean! As Josh pointed out when I got home last night,
"Mom sure is talking fast." Benadryl is definitely good for 'stream
of consciousness creativity but it's not so good on the typos!
WRITE NOW – EDIT LATER . . .

I certainly learned more about aging, patience, sympathy and a
multitude of other worthy lessons this trip. But that's not what I
want to talk about. It was such a busy two days in the ward. Not for
me but for the nurses. On the floor which houses Ob/Gyn – Maternity
and Onc/Gyn (I made that up seems to be a good short form for
Gyny oncology!) Anyway, my ward had emergency patients, like two
of my roommates who were in for other ailments. Top it off with
the "Moaner", the nurses were hopping. While the nurses were
going crazy, I busied myself with filling out the food choices for
the next day – for which will be for the next person in my bed.
It has become my secret enjoyment to provide my fellow cancer
patients with the lowest salt, lowest sugar and heaviest veggie
option on the menu. I am sure there are two people (I filled out
Della's form too) not all that happy with their Fish with herbs,
broccoli and the fruit cup instead of the Carrot cake with that
delicious icing and a lemon tea instead of coffee or regular tea.
They may curse now but perhaps it will help ;-)

As I walked around the halls to burn off some of effects my alcohol
laced chemo and my big bag of beneadryl with my now battery run
IV pole and my new name for hot flashes "power surges" it occurred
to me that my 6 year old "patent idea" perhaps needed changing.
I had been discussing with some of the engineers at work that we
could solve our battery power requirements for 8 hours of battery
use for our cordless office phones that we could solve the issue if
we could charge them with a "fat battery". Now the concept here

is calories are energy. Most of us consume "excess" calories. If we could attach a patch to a "fat" area of our body, convert the calories or fat stored in our bodies into a useable source to run the cordless phone, I figured we would have a million dollar idea. Really, think about it! What woman would not love to talk on the phone AND burn calories and fat from our butts while doing so! After yesterday, why not convert these "power surges" that many of us on the 8th floor are having? We could hold the pole and some form of conductor would convert the hot flash to a battery charging mechanism in the pump! Save batteries and find a valuable use for a "renewable" energy source. It's all good in my mind. I told my idea to a few of the nurses on the floor. They laughed and thought it was a good idea. Maybe, just maybe!

If you recall the last time I had IP Chemo it was quite difficult and took 3 nurses to insert the needle. I shared this with my nurse . . . to let her know my anxiety, and the possible swearing that could accompany her doing the same to me this time. Then she told me she had never done it. My nurse is fairly new to the ward and after 6 months on the ward she was allowed to take the IP Chemo training, and as I quickly found out that although she went through the IP Chemo training – she had never been on the right shift to get to stick the needle into the catheter. Great, a virgin! I am happy to report that with one prick it was all done! She did a great job and I didn't even swear. I told "The head chemo nurse" who was there, how well she did. Dan suggested she get a raise. They have all been so truly helpful and I will have to do something special when this is all done.

By the way, why Maternity and Cancer patients on the same floor? I wondered. I figure there are several options to why. The most obvious is that many of the doctors are gynecologists. That fits. I was thinking though the patients have something in common. I know that when I had Josh I washed my hands excessively well, many times a day to protect him from germs. As a cancer patient my diligence has gone up again with washing my hands. I wonder . . .

Again, I thank you for letting my legal drug induced thinking pour out onto my page and into your mailboxes!

Carole

February 21, 2008
Subject: Free!

Hi Guys,

They are so impressed with my drinking habits (WATER!!!) and my lack of problems with this chemo I do not need to have the 24-hour hydration through the PIC line. This makes peeing a bagillion times a day worthwhile! Freeeee from my leash!

Carole

February 26, 2008
Re: Have we met?

Hi Guys,

In for my "day only" chemo! Okay I have noticed that I am not as buzzed as with my overnight treatment. I can only assume that the whole overnight system is to ensure we don't have wacked out chemo patients driving home causing accidents!

The "Moaner" is still in her bed next door to where I am now. (Rumor has it the gig is up about her pain "level". I really want to see if they have weaned her off her "needles for pain")

The weather, well it is Tuesday in the winter of 2008, which inevitably means it snowed this morning.

The chemo room brings 3 new people. An 85-year-old woman, who lives on her own, who just finished her chemo and she is poo pooing needing a wheelchair out to the front door. Yet, I notice, how pleasant she was about it. How positive she is as she sits with a smile, framed by rosy cheeks.

The lady across the way is my age. She still has her hair or else she spent big bucks on a very long blonde wig. Her husband and her play Texas hold'em to occupy their time here. The couple are texting. In other circumstances they could be friends of ours, but like all encounters here, they are short, polite and never does anyone ask about the other's cancer "status". That must be

offered up. It seems to be that un-written cancer rule. I do learn
that I work with her brother. That will do for now – I will need
to decide if I bring this up to him, when I see him.

These types of "meetings" lead to future conversations that
start with "How do I know you? We've met." They will largely go
unresolved, I imagine. I can't think of asking someone "did we
meet in chemo?" But perhaps I am wrong and maybe this type of
conversation happens.

These things pop up in my head as I start to prepare to move from
the 'C' word and move into the 'R' stage in my life.

Carole

February 28, 2008
Re: Things I've changed

Hi Guys,

With one round of chemo left to go, things seemed to be rolling around
in my head. What things I wanted to include in these mails, possibly
in a book, as my word count nears 45,000 words. It is amazing that
I had not written a single word for myself, prior to my diagnosis,
since I was in high school and now I can accredit so many words – not
for business, not any purpose but to feel, to share and to entertain.
There are so many things that have changed in the last 5 months. You
cannot come out of this journey without a change to your soul. You
cannot come out of this without a new perspective on life.

Last summer I would have told any of you that I am a very happily
married woman who loves my son and husband. Have a wonderful,
loving extended family. A person, who loves my job, enjoys the
challenges, the camaraderie with co-workers and strong feelings
of self worth. Today I will tell you again. I love my husband
and son and family. And yes, I am looking forward to go back to
work. I do have a realization about the amount of stress I had
felt over the past year with concerns over high tech layoffs all
round and a heavy push to finally bring our company to an IPO and
a merger that I felt, could lead to "redundancies."

When I was first diagnosed, I received from Cathy, a cancer diet, and tips for managing cancer. These tips came from her aunt who is suffering from Stage 4 cancer. She wrote the "tips" in 2005 and is still going strong today. I took heed. Just reviewing these tips, I looked at the last one . . . it says, "Everyone who is seriously ill needs to look at an emotional imbalance. Illness starts in your head, even if you do not realize it."

When I started writing this book, I thought this illness came to me, perhaps, because I have been longing and searching for where my faith lies. For several years I have been reading, searching to find something – an answer in the form of religion, lack of religion, spirituality, faith, my acorn . . . something. Now through many, many coincidences, opportunities, kismet, serendipity, faith, focus and many long hours of introspective thought, on-line cathartic emails, laughs and giggles, I know what has changed and why this illness came to me. When I started this journey, I never really truly knew how many people out there were so close to me. My change; is my appreciation for all my wonderful community of friends. I have spent my life always feeling like I was somewhat of an outsider on the edge of "sisterhood". This was my own doing. This was a waste of such wonderful relationships that I already had . . . but never really appreciated how lucky I am to have all of you. I am so overwhelmed. I think I have been very fortunate to have discovered friendships new and old that fill my heart and discovered it while renewing my love of writing and sharing and discovering it with all of you. (By the way, the first "book" I ever wrote was in grade 6. I still have the hand written 25-page manuscript that I entitled "Together As One", coincidentally it too was about my friendships at the time.)

Just recently I met Jake Cole, who is running federally for the Green Party of Canada. He is the party's health critic. We are very like-minded, in that we both feel the health system must focus on prevention as well. He said something that resonated well with me. They treat you for cancer and send you on your way. If you don't change anything about your life – no wonder it comes back. Wow, very insightful. It seems simplistic but true. This has been an inspiration for me.

Last Monday at yoga, focusing on my breathing and inwardly chanting my intention "This Cancer is Gone" and thinking should I change my intention to "Keep this Cancer Gone" a thought quickly popped in my head. It told me I am doing everything right and I will beat this moving forward. And fully and completely I felt relief. It was very strange. It was very reassuring. I feel good about this. As I review all my life changes – I keep re-reviewing them to keep things going so well. I keep reviewing the list to ensure I don't forget them. Is that silly? How can I forget? Wait! That's me last summer. Now I know. I can list them all here, share them and count on you to help keep me on track in case I forget!

Major changes to keep cancer away:

1. Cruciferous vegetables every day – especially broccoli (first food I've seen mentioned to specifically state it fights ovarian cancer cells)
2. Beans, lentils, nuts, apples, blueberries, turmeric and the loads of other cancer fighting phytochemicals! Green Drink it is!
3. No sugar, no salt (okay limited . . . very limited)
4. Very little corn, rice, pasta, wheat
5. Fish and chicken better than the rest! These keep your system alkaline. Cancer thrives in a high acidic environment. Who cares if they have no hard and fast scientific confirmation that it is true? What I can tell you is that I measured my pH when they pumped me full of chemo and my system was SOOOO alkaline it was crazy. This diet keeps my body slightly alkaline . . . the chemo drops it considerably lower. So this diet is like a healthy daily dose of prevention, where chemo is the blast to try to stabilize it. Here's another way to look at it. If you have a pool you'll quickly understand this analogy. We are over 70% water . . . our pool is water. You need to keep the pH level in the 7.0 range to keep it clean and not hurt your eyes. Pool owners know that once the balance of the water goes awry the sand filter system (like our kidneys, liver and pancreas) has a hard time keeping the algae at bay. Eventually the algae take over and you need to take drastic action of clean out the algae (super chlorination). Think of the algae in a pool like cancer. It's there, in small quantities. You can't see it. It doesn't affect the pool. It's only when the balance of the water runs amuck that problems start. Keep

your body's pH in check . . . don't you think? Look how well
I have done throughout all of this!

6. No Parabens (they mimic estrogen and are carcinogenic)
7. No SLS and no "petroleum based" products on my body.
    Read labels . . . there are no hard and fast regulations on
    cosmetic products, soaps etc.
8. No plastics in the Kitchen or near your mouth . . . again there
    is a difference between what the government says is "safe" vs
    a "risk". Lead was okay 20 years ago!
9. Exercise and outdoors – cancer hates oxygen!
10. Breathe . . . long slow deep breaths daily, outside if possible.
    Yoga and meditation are great!
11. Epsom Salt in the bath – they cleanse the lymph nodes
12. Give back to the planet. We are all connected and it needs
    our help.
13. Put things in perspective . . . after cancer what could be
    worse?
14. Be Positive. Be Happy. These are things you can control. As
    someone said "You cannot control other's actions, you can only
    control your reaction to their actions" or something like
    that!
15. Always count on your family and friends. Be open and share – the
    rewards are so much better then feeling you can do it all
    yourself!

Lucky huh, I have a long lifetime of paying all of you back for
all you have done!

Thanks,

Carole

February 28, 2008
Subject: Girls Cottage Weekend!

Okay girls,

I know it is February and we have snow up to our, 'you know what's,'
but I thought it would be good to have something to look forward
to. Mark June 6th and 7th on your calendars. Rick is off on his
annual guys golf trip (which saves me the guilt of kicking him

out of the cottage for the weekend, guilt, what guilt) so I have declared that weekend girls weekend at the cottage. Both nights, one night, whatever works for everyone! Although Sandra, I have to remind you that Carole has spent the winter researching foods, environment and man made products that are bad for your health, so you may want to get there early and be prepared to take notes but I promise you I will have a beer for breakfast for you, along with my prune yogurt, hemp seed mixture.

Hope everyone can make it. I will be in touch. I'm sure as the time approaches, there will be many emails exchanged.

Love to all,

Gwen

February 28, 2008
Subject Girls Cottage Weekend

Hi Gwen,

Count me in! So let me get this though . . . Prunes and Beer for breakfast (okay I don't even eat prunes but hey I'm game ;-) but Sandra has requested nothing healthy or good for us for the whole weekend, so "we can pretend we are still young." I think I have the solution Blueberry margaritas! . . . No, no Sandra, blueberries are not good for you . . . no limes . . . bad stuff . . . yes of course they will have tequila in them! LOL. Despite all my changes . . . it's all about balance and enjoying life . . . a girls' weekend at the cottage is definitely cause for a little "balance"!
Can't wait!

Carole

March 3, 2008
Re: Spring is in the Air!

Hi Guys,

This is a first. I am outside taking a walk writing this.

My walk got delayed, because, for the first time since November, my big fury hat with the pull down ear flaps, (thanks for suggesting I buy it Sally!) seems way to warm, even for my baldish head. My scarf comes off and gloves in pocket. Now I am set to take a walk on this first spring like day in 2008. There is no breeze, the early morning freezing rain has melted and unlike the last few months where it seemed like it was, snowing or very cold, today is both warm and sunny. Nice fresh air. Sorry Oprah, I may have to miss you today! I guess getting out for a walk on a early spring afternoon is one of the perks I shall enjoy for a while.

Thrill yourself everyday!

Now, if I can learn to type on this blackberry, while walking and step over the dog poop on the street, everything will work out just fine!

Carole

March 10, 2008
Subject: Here it comes . . .

Hi Guys,

It has been a while. My mother in law asked if I had removed her from the "Hi Guys" list since it had been so long since my last mail. Forewarned is forearmed . . . tomorrow morning I go to my last overnight stay for Chemo. Based on the very early morning (made worse by the time change last weekend!) and the Benadryl and alcohol laced chemo . . . beware you may see a full mailbox tomorrow full of drug induced ranting, raves and observations of the cancer process!

After tomorrow, I go again next Tuesday for a 'day' chemo treatment then I am done! Well, okay, they need to remove the PIC line, remove the catheter from my rib cage and a final meeting with the doctor, and then CA125 blood tests for the next MANY, MANY years . . . but basically I am done . . . cause I don't plan to have to do this again. The OHIP funded drug induced inspiration stops and I will need to rely on my own devices to finish up this book with witty and inspirational observations!

Carole

PS okay you nurses on my list . . . I have heard PIC, PICC, PIK what is it? I need to get it right for the final draft of the book.

PPS I am reading *In Defense of Food* by Michael Pollan and it gives me hope that I am on the right track to keeping this cancer GONE!

March 11, 2008
Subject: Drug Free Observation

Hi Guys,

Well we made it in early to the hospital due to the fact that for the first time it's not snowing!

So I have a semi private room. After the last two overnight chemo treatments, I have learned to pack ear plugs, bring instant coffee as you never get enough in the little brown cup that comes with breakfast, bring my own fruit and nuts for healthy snacks, bring earphones that cover my whole ears to block out the TV blaring from my roommate whom seems hard of hearing and seems to have lost her earplugs or is simply sharing!

I have also learned that if at all possible to get a window bed. I seem to have a common pet peeve when flying. I always get a window seat when flying. I like to look out - still! I always get pissed off when I don't get the window seat and person who did shuts the blind and blocks the sun, the clouds, and the light! I think the window seat person has an obligation to share. I think this rule

applies to hospital beds. If you are fortunate enough to get a
window bed you, need to share the sun, it makes you smile!

Carole

March 11, 2008
Subject: Where's my hit

Hi Guys,

Still no drugs! It is March break and they're down a nurse. In the
interim Dan just got back from getting me another Tim's coffee.
Thank God for legal stimulants. Upon his return first thing I
notice was that the front of his dress shirt was un-tucked and
hanging down in front of his crotch. I pointed, "Did you forget
to check?" "Oh no! It's been out all the way to Tim's." which is
8 floors down, through the long halls of the regular cancer wing,
and over to the new addition of the critical care wing . . .
basically as far a walk as possible, within the hospital. Dan's
saddened face looks up after tucking in, "and I thought I was
looking hot since I got a lot of stares!" Ahhh :-(then he adds,
"I guess it's just elderly ladies from now on."
The two of us laughed for at least 5 minutes solid! Much better
than coffee or Benadryl!

Carole

March 11, 2008
Subject: Conspiracy Theory Trilogy

Hi Guys,

I know. I thought I would have rattled off an email by now.

Can you believe it? I fell asleep. Finally, the typical Benadryl reaction, sleep! Thank the time change and early morning for helping out. Perhaps it's the long known ancient remedy for sleep that helped. I was reading!

I started reading *In Defense of Food*. A non-fiction book about, well, the emergence of "food like" products, and their impact on our health, what science, the lobbyists and what the government have done to impact their proliferation. To me it reads like a bestseller. A page-turner that you can't put down! To me it reads of hope, taking back control.

Next on the list I have ordered *Cancer: 101 Solutions to a Preventable Epidemic*. The second installment on my conspiracy thriller trilogy! I wonder if there is a third one on the cosmetic industry called "Through the Skin; Poisoning You, One lash at a time" or perhaps "Killing Me Softly: our Quest for Younger Skin" (I think there is really a book called "Don't go to the Cosmetic Store without this Book) and a forth one the called "This Clean House: why Wall Street is Clean, Not Green or how about "Who Paid the Way to the Whitehouse . . . Why the Petroleum Industry Gains from the all the Fictitious books listed above"

Okay lots of sarcasm and cynicism. I'm not that bad, but it is prudent to recognize that big business (food processors, the cosmetics industry and cleaning product companies) has weight with what the government says about scientific research. Which, if beneficial to industry the government will much more easily support a claim . . . such that "Frito Lays chips get a green health check mark because their baked chips has 0 Trans fat in them now – BUT THEY ARE CHIPS!! Whereas the government may tend to not support a claim, that is bad for big business. On the other end of the scale they say that there is not enough research to claim that coal tar in our shampoo – a known carcinogen – doesn't require a warning label . . . because I guess most people don't, wash, rinse, **repeat** and its that second wash day after day for 60 years actually builds up enough in our systems to cause cancer! Dam, I am getting cynical again and I wanted to end on a high note!

Well looks like I have loads of inspiration for future books! So much to do, LOADS of time to do it in!!

Carole

March 11, 2008
Subject: Un-avoidable Meeting

Hi Guys,

My roommate left this morning. Another roommate came in this evening. She also has ovarian cancer. She went through her first session in 2006. She is back. Her CA125 was 3 one month. 3 months later she was 40, and then she came into emergency with fluid, bloating, constipation etc. Just like my symptoms in Sept. She is now at a CA 125 of 90. She looks pregnant? I was at 3335 and looked pregnant? Anyway, I have been avoiding this type of conversation all along . . . but to avoid this would be rude. I listened and hoped to learn. She is retired. I am guessing in her late 60's. When she was done her first round, she went back to life as usual. She and her husband travelled. Then I got my courage up. I had to ask but like a lawyer I only wanted to ask if I knew the answer in advance. "Did you change your diet?"
"No." We drank good wine we ate great! We must enjoy these things," she and her husband replied filling in the sentence together. That was the answer I wanted. It gives me hope. She too had an easy time of it when she first did her 6 rounds of chemo. Darn.
"Have you had any recent stresses?" "No."
"You didn't notice anything before the last two weeks?" "No, just little twinges."
"It crept up again?" Huummm
This is going to be tough! Her husband did say that I could ask my GP to get a CA125 test monthly if I want. It sounds like the standard is every three months.

No coincidences. This encounter with Jacelyne who is where she is today is a needed step for me to double my resolve!

This brings me back to my weird statement that there is comfort in chemo . . . and now the chase is on. I got a head start on the bear, with my 15 rules I sent out earlier, I know I can outrun him!

Carole

March 12, 2008
Subject: Elevated Status

Hi Guys,

I just got off the phone with Dan. We have been playing "The Insurance Game" with our insurance company. They are the insurance carrier on our line of credit with the bank. We have been filling out forms and my doctors have been filling out forms since October. The insurance I pay covers loss of job and illness. Last August I figured I would get this insurance because, I was worried about lay offs and wanted the coverage for that and thought it was a responsible, proactive thing to do. Again, call it divine intervention or what have you, I didn't need it for a layoff but the medical coverage came in handy when I got my diagnosis at the end of Sept.

Hold that thought while I tell you about my other proactive, responsible thing I did. When I went for my physical in June I asked Dr. White, my GP for an ultrasound for ovarian cancer as I thought I was at higher risk. I had no symptoms. I just figured it was proactive. I got the test and it came back negative.

Okay.

So let's go back to the insurance company. According to my policy, they should have been paying my line of credit since Oct. They haven't. It's a good thing we can afford it. Thanks in part to a wonderful benefit package through my work. This morning the insurance company declined my claim due to, get this, because I requested the ultrasound in June, they deemed it is a pre-existing condition. So, being responsible for my own health, being proactive I am being declined. Oh and of course, perhaps they think I am a psychic. Hummm, perhaps I will change my title to Dr. Carole McCaskill, psychic oncologist.

We will get my GP to fax the negative test result. I knew they would delay paying. I am not a lawyer but I am smart enough to know that when push comes to shove asking your GP for a test, does not a diagnosis make! Think of the impact on all those hypochondriacs.

Ahhhh,
Carole

(Update: They finally did pay . . . after my GP sent them several notes about how my concerns . . . are just concerns not a diagnosis! Thanks, Dr. White!)

March 12, 2008
Subject: Party All the time

Hi Guys,

So once again my party life has prepared me for chemo. The nurse, as part of the routine, reads the doctor's 'orders' and compares it to the bag of chemo to make sure they are injected me with the right poison! Today, the nurse looked up from the chemo bag and said in disbelief, "we haven't reduced the strength of your Cisplatin?" Cisplatin is a VERY strong chemo, stronger than many of the others, causing nausea, vomiting etc. of which I have had none on the other two rounds. The first round of this Cisplatin treatment, they gave me 3 days of hydration via my PICC line. Last time I mentioned my distain for the 24 hour pumping of the hydration and they said I have done so well with no side effects I didn't need it. So last round no hydration, no side effects! Well we all know that anyone who wants to party and drink the night away must fully hydrate themselves – even alternating drinks with glasses of water. I have an acute sense of this equation and have been diligent in drinking lots of water!

So today when she was a bit shocked that they kept the strength
of my chemo at the max level all this seemed to fit. Loads of
hydration (a well learned lesson over many years of parties) and
they worried about my abdomen feeling burning because of the
chemo. Well let me tell you there have been many nights where my
stomach felt burning more than this. One Halloween party comes to
mind where I figured cutting lemons in half, sticking my thumb in
the center to create a hole! Filling it with tequila and topping
it with salt was such a novel way to do a tequila shooter I must
have had at least 5 or 6 - you want to feel burning in your
stomach and nausea the next morning - now we can talk! Of course
I took the max quantity of chemo - I didn't train all these year
to wimp out now!

Carole

March 12, 2008
Subject: RE: Party all the time!

Hi Carole,

Oh my GOD, ten words into this story and I was WAAAAAAAy ahead
of you to the tequila/lemon story! It's not everyone who has her
very own tequila dispenser you know . . . ! LOL (For those of
you who don't know, she does) I'm thinking that we may have to
shoot one more round, heavy on the lemons, LOW on the salt, and
raise our glasses with a "F** You" salute to all of this . . .
of course there will be gagging, burning, and generally shouting
much profanity as we throw our glasses on the floor and stomp them
into pieces.

A final farewell salute!!
(only for you my dear, because the very smell of it, makes me gag)

Warmest Regards,
Sonya

Benadryl and Blackberry Alert

March 12, 2008
Subject: RE: RE: Party all the time!
Cc: Hi Guys

Hi Sonya,

Perhaps I will at the summer solstice. I haven't (touched tequila in years but I could make an obsession)

Carole

March 12, 2008
Subject: RE: Party all the time!
Cc: Hi Guys

Hi Carole,

Uh, oh. It's kicking in . . . Did you mean obsession or exception? :-)

Patti

Cc: Hi Guys
Subject: RE: Party all the time!
CC: Hi Guys

Hi Patti

Yes . . . I meant exception not obsession! That could be the drugs or that "mistake" could be a Freudian slip! LOL Carole

March 12, 2008
Subject: RE: Party all the time!
CC: Hi Guys

Too funny!!

Patti

March 14, 2008
Subject: Talk about protection

Hi Guys,

This email has been rated "R" for sexual content . . . you have
been warned!

So here's the thing. When I started the IP Chemo, they suggested
that Dan wear a condom during sex. So first of all, aside from a
belly full of at least 4 liters of fluid, making me feel somewhat
"bloated" – think of it like being pregnant in your second trimester.
Then add the fact that most of the "plumbing" is gone and one would
imagine a wide open door into my abdomen (I assume it was sealed
off??) Couple that with the nurses wearing protective gloves, gowns
when they are handling the chemo and witnessing a burn hole in another
patients quilt when a "splash" of chemo hit it . . . do they really
think a thin piece of latex is going to protect a man's favorite
part of their body??? I don't know but somehow I think that warning
is enough to scare most people off, but hey, who knows . . . this is
one of those things that never gets discussed . . . only by me! ;-)

Carole

March 18, 2008
Subject: Mixed emotions

Hi Guys,

Here I am, sitting in an all too familiar room. Receiving my last
dose of Benadryl, in preparation for my last dose of taxol via
the catheter attached to my ribs. The worry about being poked in
the ribs with a needle is gone. The concern about my reaction to

the chemo is gone. It has become part of a routine. It means my white count is low – be careful for a few weeks.

My hair will start to come back in a few weeks – slowly but surely. What is new is the future. I have been realizing that as strange as it sounds, there is "comfort in chemo". During treatment you have tangible results and feedback – reassurance that the cancer is regressing – perhaps leaving altogether. I get reassurance from the blood tests that things are going as they should. Every three weeks – a checkpoint!

After today my visits will be in three-month increments. Now I am left to my own devices to keep it away. For me, I think it is based on food. For me I think eliminating processed food laden with soy, a source of phytoestrogen. Will this work? Is it scientifically proven? No. But you need something to pin your hopes on. There are other changes too. The toughest one will be finding a balance between remembering I am living with cancer – and as such proactively doing what I can versus over focusing on it. I look forward to the future. One day at a time.

Carole

March 18, 2008
Subject: Not Alone

Hi Guys,

I just finished talking to Lynn, the "training" nurse. She has been extremely helpful along the way.

When talking today, she is looking at setting up some workshops and support for people entering the post treatment phase. It seems that many people have questions, concerns about "going it alone". I am going to send her some of my mails to help support her bid for funding for a fellowship to pull a support package together. I have offered my opinion when she gets the funding! Like I needed her permission to offer my opinion! LOL. It is nice to think that my mood is "normal" and good to hear that there is a need to look at post treatment and that it's not just me!

Carole

March 20, 2008
Subject: Reflections

Hi Guys,

This transition seems to be a time for reflection . . . these reflections seem to be coming in the middle of the night . . . I assume things will settle down as I get used to this new phase . . .

Reflecting back on the past 6 months, I realized something that although "inferred" throughout my emails, has never been mentioned directly. There is something for which I must state my appreciation. I have talked before about how lucky we are in Canada to have universal medical coverage. This is truly a distinction between Canada and many other countries. That can only truly be appreciated when faced with a chronic, life threatening health problem. I have always been appreciative and have espoused how this makes Canada a much better place to live than many other countries. Along this journey I have seen many people less financially fortunate that me . . . yet, they received the same medical attention as me. I have also witnessed a billionaire, receiving the same medical coverage as me . . . ah.

On further reflection I have also come to appreciate my employer. I work at Mitel. I have been at Mitel for 28 years this month. (I know! I started when I was 10 . . . I'm not that old – really!) Over the years at Mitel I have seen many changes. I often tell people that I grew up at Mitel . . . who has done some growing too.

When I was in my 20's the best benefit of working at Mitel was the social life. In the 80's life was great at Mitel. There were parties, whether organized by Mitel to celebrate some milestone or to just show employee appreciation or whether it was a Friday get together with myriad young people everywhere. In the 90's as I grew and the company grew I appreciated the opportunity to grow. The challenge of working hard and receiving reward! I felt no bounds up to Y2K. After 911 and the dot.com bust, things have changed. No one can deny it. Change is a constant. This is sometimes tough, but for me, I feel it is just another challenge.

A company is a growing living entity. Just as a person is . . . so why not grow and change?

In many of my observations of people going through their cancer treatments, I have felt they are much less fortunate than me. Absolutely number one is the support system I have. Friends and family have made this an easier journey for me than for many. There is another reason though. The day I was diagnosed I was able to go on short-term disability. This allowed me to go through my treatment without having to worry about a loss of income. (Every month when I go in for treatment I get a questionnaire that asks about my "financial" situation and other stressors . . . I have none.) I also have benefited from a drug plan and medical benefits that have allowed me to get drugs cheaper than many, semi – private, private rooms at the hospital and on and on.

When you hear a "value" that these benefits add to your income. You may not appreciate it. Like me in the past, you may have thought – give me the money instead of the benefit . . . Hopefully you will never fully have to appreciate having these benefits as much as I have. There is nothing like a safety net when you need it. There is nothing like the Canadian spirit of helping others in need. If you have benefits and don't need them – remember that when your company opts to provide benefits available to all – you are helping someone who really needs it! (I just stepped down off my high horse . . . sorry)

Carole

March 25, 2008
Subject: Spreading the word

Hi Guys,

My home nurse asked me several weeks ago if I would mind phoning another patient of hers who is in her 20's, who also has cancer and is not doing so well. I called and spoke to her mom, who needs to come over every day to help her since she was not eating and not feeling well. She was in bed asleep. So I told her mom about how my diet changes, (low sodium, no sugar, little wheat and lots of veggies), my vitamins and about how my green drink had helped me.

Her mother wrote down all the information. Today she called me back and wanted to thank me. After talking to me, she went out and got her daughter the nine-bean soup mix base I use daily and added all the veggies to it. They changed some of their high sodium options, switched to less red meat and natural soaps and cleansers as I had suggested. She said that after one meal of my soup her daughter felt much better.

She told me her daughter said, "She saved my life" (meaning me :-). I'm not so sure about that, but I do believe that her daughter finally felt that she had some control, she had something to focus on . . . and in the end, her mother said she feels great now! It feels good and I am glad I helped. I just sent her an email with other information and added that I wrote out my feelings and experiences in my emails to my friends. Now I really want to get this book published . . . . almost time to edit!

Carole

March 28, 2008
Subject: Its all in the Punctuation mark?.!

Hi Guys,

So I am now 3 days past my 21-day cycle of chemo. My white count is rebuilding, my poor little hair follicles are starting to rebound and I begin my journey into the world of remission. When I look back on the past 6 months there are 3 words that have kept popping up. When I was first diagnosed a friend said "Why not me?"

At the time, I didn't think too much about it. A few weeks later when the reality was starting to set in, the words popped into my head again. When the fact that I have cancer moved from "surreal" to reality, it struck me, cancer hits so many people, "Why not me."

Now I begin the transition into remission and I begin to face the fear of keeping the cancer gone. Using all the knowledge I've researched about diet and lifestyle changes that I've incorporated

into my life. I look at those three words again and use them to
focus on beating the odds of recurrence . . . "Why not me!"

Carole

April 1, 2008
Subject: Return to Sender

Hi Guys,

They keep sending me stuff. Medical stuff! Extra gauze, alcohol
wipes trays for caring for my PIC line. I must have about $1000
worth of stuff in my front hall. I have made a few phone calls. I
want to ensure that OHIP doesn't get billed for all this stuff.
I can't really find where to return it. I have phoned around and
it seems a bit unclear if anyone knows how to get this stuff back
into the system and get a credit for OHIP. Well, in the end I
got the medical supply company to pick up the extra stuff. I can
only hope that it somehow gets credited back to OHIP. Perhaps I
am an April fool!

Carole

April 3, 2008
Subject: Full Circle

Hi Guys,

What a great day! We just bought a new car, a hybrid. I got it
yesterday. Driving it is a stress relief. It was expensive but
here's my rationale. I looked at the car as a capital investment
with a fixed expense rate over 5 years. The variable expense is the
gas. More than likely going up! The car will meet my needs with
the best gas millage. It allows me to stop looking at gas prices
from gas station to gas station. It allows me to stop wondering
which day of the week gas prices will be at their lowest. It will
allow me to enjoy my country drive into work and back home. It
will allow me to forget that salaries are not keeping pace with
the increases in gas. It is one less thing that will relieve
stress. Is my expensive car a luxury? I think not. It makes feel

good about doing something for the environment. It makes me feel good about reducing the amount of money going to the coffers of gas companies and having my dollars speak, and all this, with stress relief. I'd say it was quite a wise investment.

So, new car, a great lunch with Kristin, a long time friend, 8 degrees ABOVE zero, and I am sitting here waiting at the General, waiting for the pre operative work in preparation for that last bit of evidence (the catheter attached to my ribs) to be removed in day surgery in a week.

It was 6 months ago that I was sitting here getting X-rays and blood tests to confirm my diagnosis. It was 6 months ago that I saw a woman in the waiting room reading a book by Ivan E Coyote. Dan mentioned to the woman that we had just met Ivan and that she was a neighbor. It was 6 months ago that I formed a new friendship with Ivan. It was 6 months ago that I knew that Ivan E Coyote – an award winning author, moved into little old Fitzroy Harbour, stopped in at the Harbour Store when the coffee club was 'in session', and thereby came into my life as inspiration to write a book.

Is it coincidence as well, that the woman that was reading Ivan's book six months ago, is a friend of the Emcee who introduced Ivan at a recent storytelling gig? Is it coincidence that the woman mentioned "the lady in the waiting room at the General" that she had met, happened to be the same "lady with cancer" that Ivan mentions in one of her stories? Is it even coincidence that Ivan came into Fitzroy when I started this journey and that she is leaving at the end . . . almost to the day? Is it coincidence that a coyote is a power animal that is part of North American Indian's Shamanism, that the coyote is inspiration in this belief? Are all these things coincidental? I think not.

Is there truth to the "6 degrees of separation" theory? That somehow we are all connected? That what each of us does, impacts all of us? That impacts nature? That things happen for a reason? That everything that happens to us is a journey, that is part of who we are and what we will become?

I think so.

Carole.

April 5, 2008
Subject: Wigs 'n things

Hi Guys,

Ahhhh, this is my first email of 2008 written to you and sent wirelessly from my front porch. Gotta love high tech! It is 13 degrees and all I need is a light jacket and a hat. As the weather gets warmer and hiding my bald head under a warm toque becomes less and less an option, is making it seem like my hair is extremely slow coming back. It has only been about 4 weeks since my last chemo session and I know, they told me it takes 3 weeks for the chemo to leave your system, therefore my poor little hair follicles have only had one week of growth. But I have high expectations of them. I expect my hair to be at least covering my entire head very soon, if only 1/16th of an inch or some similar metric measurement that I never quick figured out!

I am now wearing a ball cap, which is great, except that you can tell I am bald. I tried on my Mom's French beret a while back but unfortunately it only made me look like a bald Girl Guide. I bought a really cute straw hat with an exceptionally wide brim aka Julie Roberts in Pretty Woman at the polo match . . . however with snow on the ground that does not seem to be a viable option either! I bought a "Gillian" type rain hat, which covers my head sufficiently to mask my lack of hair – but without rain that would seem to draw attention as well. What to do?

I was brave last Thursday night. I went to our Fitzroy Harbour Community Association Annual General Meeting, without my wig and sporting my winter hat, which got too warm so I switched to my ball cap. Upon becoming a member of the executive I was called to the front with the rest of the executive for a picture for our local newspaper. In a moment of panic I grabbed my winter hat stuck it on my head . . . now I have to face total strangers staring at my picture in next week's paper . . . wondering who the idiot is, wearing a winter hat in a building . . . oh well such is life.

Today I went to the Rural Summit Meeting in the city to discuss – well, rural issues. I opted to wear my wig. I figured it was a much better option. It was a good plan, poorly executed. I should know better, I am not good waking up early without coffee in my system.

I adjusted the little clippy things that tighten my wig to hold
it on. (Remember I have no hair to attach any bobby pins to hold
it down - which the wig lady told me after I stupidly asked the
question about using bobby pins to hold it on . . . this I learned
last fall LOL!) Well, I guess I tightened it a bit too tight. There
I was sitting down smiling at Mayor Larry O'Brian, Federal MP Pierre
Poliver, Ken Kirkpatrick, the media, several other notable Ottawa
politicians, and about 300 people all smiling and getting to know
each other. I am talking to a uniformed Police Officer, engrossed
in a lively discussion about the merits, or lack thereof, of urban
planning in rural Ottawa and my wig begins slipping up my forehead.
I am sure during the 5 minute conversation my forehead grew about
an inch before his eyes, and yes off course the top of my head had
to have grown about that much as well - since the wig had to go
somewhere!!! In all the times wearing my wig I have never felt it
move so much, so quickly! As I stood there I figured - stop moving
my arms - this may help, but if you've seen me talk passionately
about something - you know this is difficult. Then I stopped moving
my face quite so much - this too could help . . . The urge to
pull the wig down was overwhelming at this point. This cop is
good though. I saw no weird expressions, no telltale signs of
"what the hell is happening to her hair" type eye movements. I
couldn't stand it anymore. I needed to find an eloquent way to end
the conversation. There is no break in chatter. I don't want to
be rude. Perhaps I am imagining this whole wig thing, I thought.
Suddenly a man walks up and says to the cop "I need to talk to
you" . . . I took the opening. Said thanks and good-bye! I walked
through the crowd, around the corner and yanked my wig down. It
had gotten so high that I could feel the breeze tickling my sparse
little feather like hairs on my head. LOL . . . .

Perhaps I will find a spring hat . . . perhaps I will be patient
enough to wait a few more weeks until my hair is spread even over
my head, and at a number 1 on the razor setting. That reminds
me - I will have to tell Dude - who cut my hair last October that
her cut was the best value I have ever had - can you imagine 1
hair cut lasting 6 months! ;-)

Hats and Wigs and things - who cares? The warm weather is here
after a LONG Hard winter!! Happy spring!

Carole

April 10, 2008
Subject: Be the Change you wish to see in the world!

Hi Guys,

It was always a joke of mine about some of the exposure I have had in my past . . . such as painting my finger nails with liquid paper – the old formulation that had a carcinogen in it (Who knew . . . I was 18 years old!) Like working on an assembly line with lead fumes going up my nose, drinking and eating while working with the lead on my hands and on occasion I chewed on it. (D'oh!) All lead solder has been removed from my company's products about 25 years later . . . due to UK and European Union requirements. And last but not least the Trichloroethylene that we used to clean the solder spills and I used to remove dirt from my hands. Did that impact me now 25 years later? Who knows? I only worked in that environment for about a year. The reason this is important to speak about is because back in the early 80's these were things that were all "fine" to use. Remember this as I harp on some of the newer "suspect" products, like SLS, Parabens, plastics and other petroleum based chemicals found in our cosmetics, cleaning products and yes even "food like" products that the government is "reviewing" today. It brings new meaning to buyer beware eh?

Take a look. Perhaps taking a little preventative measures are a great idea for you . . . changing your spending habits will force manufacturers and the government to take a quicker, closer, safer road. Your dollar is your power. Use it for your health and the health of the planet.

Carole

April 13, 2008
Subject: Wiggin' out!

Hi Cathy and Sonya,

Thanks so much supporting me in my short hair experience. I hope you don't regret shaving your hair so short! It looks wonderful on both of you. What will they think of the 3 of us when we hit

the Carp farmer's market and garden centers this spring! I know
they will not suspect cancer . . . they may think we are a very
strange, middle-aged "gang" of women . . . belonging to some cult!
Maybe people always think that about us anyway. LOL.

Carole

April 14, 2008
Subject: One more Hurdle

Hi Guys,

Today was a second to final trip to the General in this odyssey! There was no snow on our trip today . . . it seems spring has finally come, although it was very cold at 5:30 this morning. Today I had day surgery to remove the catheter attached to my ribs. All in all it was very easy. I avoided the 1/2 hour long discussion with the Anesthesiologist by avoiding drinking lemon tea . . . since I mistakenly thought it qualified as a clear liquid for my surgery in December :-) The surgery today was very quick and easy and I have steri-strips instead of stitches.

Tomorrow is my final appointment at the cancer clinic. I assume they tell me about, 3 month checks and I get to bombard them with questions (as you all know I will) about a new load of vitamins I have recently researched, any medical community support for any "alternative" therapy's I have investigated. I am not going to ask my prognosis. If they tell me okay. If they don't I am thinking I don't want to ask . . . this question will undoubtedly cause a lack of sleep.

Today . . . there are two things for certain – tomorrow symbolized the first day of the rest of my life . . . oh how this expression holds to true for this occasion, and second, tomorrow will be the last (perhaps several emails) to my "Hi Guys" list . . . tomorrow I begin to edit. It is a very funny thing. Today there was a lady just starting her treatment and my nurse, who noted how positive I was, and how concerned this new patient was, casually stated to me how "there are some things I could tell her." I responded with "actually, I wrote a book". She asked what my main message was. I told her it was "to be positive and that the book took a lighter, sometimes funny approach to my experiences." This was funny because it was my first time telling a complete stranger that I wrote a book. It felt funny, but it felt good.

Carole

April 15, 2008
Subject: Wig worries coming true!

Hi Guys,

Dan and I were just driving down the 417 on our way to the General and my wig worries from last fall nearly came true. I had been wondering if my wig would withstand the wind from an open car window at 120km/hr. Well, we just passed a car with a dirty back window. Instead of someone writing the traditional "wash me", someone wrote, "I suck dick" (sorry if I offended) and they drew a picture to accompany the statement. It was just what Dan and I needed! We broke out into laughter. Dan pulled up beside him, slowed down and rolled down my window. Holding my hair I yelled, "Wash your window, it says, "I suck dick"." He smiled and laughed. I'm not sure if he caught everything I said. Either he will wash his window or he will be thinking about me later! (Because I did look hot in my wig and leather coat and new shades) either way laughter is always great and testing out my wig security in that manner was perfect – even if I am about to retire it! More after my appointment!

Carole

April 15, 2008
Subject: RE: Wig worries coming true!
CC: Hi Guys

Hi Carole,

What was Patrick doing on the 417? (Sorry if I offended) :)

Tim

April 15, 2008
Subject: RE: Wig worries coming true!
CC: Hi Guys

Hi Carole,

hahahahaaaaa that so made me laugh.
You are the Best.

Dianne

. . . . Just read Tim's email . . . and that really made me laugh . . . .

D

April 15, 2008
Re: Do a little dance . . .

Hi Guys,

My appointment today was with Dr, Fung Ke Fung. When this adventure began I started with trying to meet with him. I ended up meeting the rest of his team, who are all wonderful. Now on my last day, I meet him. No wonder he has a wonderful team. (He heads up the Gyny/Oncology Dept.) He is absolutely terrific. He was wonderful at answering my questions – in fact he was great at articulating my questions for me, as it seemed a bit of blathering was coming out of my mouth as I rushed to try to get all my questions out, in what I thought would be a short time I would have with him. In fact it turns out my appointment was supposed to be moved out but didn't - yet he fit me in anyway and I never felt rushed at all!

So his name sounds like a disco band from the 80's. His demeanor does make you want to 'do a little dance', a happy dance which Dan and I will be doing next week, since Dan signed us up for ballroom/Latin dance lessons!

Carole

April 15, 2008
Subject: Summer Solstice!

Hi Guys,

This year summer solstice is officially on June 20th. You are all invited. It is a Friday and it starts at 7pm. Bring a beverage, a snack and your bathing suit.

As the longest day of the year, to mark off the official party season, and as a mystical day for old pagan religions, wiccans and other groups that worship the Goddess, this day is the perfect time to hold an all female celebration.

We tell the men that we are all scantily clad in white gauze dresses and dance around my pool filled with lighted candles and recite incantations. Really, you can wear whatever you want, we do light candles but the only incantations come from the lips of my friends' somewhat fuzzy minds after a beverage or two!

We begin the night with a tradition I started to help fill my garden. Each year I ask all my friends that attend to plant a flower in my garden. (I supply the flowers) Every time I am out in my garden that year I think of all my friends. My flower garden is now overflowing with flowers . . .

We enjoy a night of laughs, sitting in the hot tub or taking a swim. We connect; we celebrate the coming summer and our friendships.

I look forward to seeing all of you to celebrate all that is the Goddess. The strength of women, the power of to give life, and the power to overcome all obstacles that come our way!

Carole

April 15, 2008
Subject: RE: Summer Solstice!

Cc Hi Guys,

Carole? OMG June huh? What is a boy to wear? White gauze right? Shit . . . black is so slimming. You know Carole, white gauze is not so cheap when you're trying to cover a whale? Dam, it's going to cling to my fat old ass (pause for thought) I'm going to need to find someone who does, bikini waxing . . . along with back, crack and love handles (I'll have to take a week off for that). White gauze gown huh? I wonder if Duct tape holds in water??? I'll have to "phone a friend."

We're hitting BBQ season so a diet is off the table. My mother in-law has a Gazelle stored here; maybe I could dangle a spring roll from the ceiling just out of reach. Come to think of it, if it didn't work for the in-law, it probably won't work for me. Which reminds me; please don't fill the hot tub up to much. When I get in, the cup tends to runneth over.

Now we all know I have loads of hair with a crop circle in the centre . . . so a bathing cap is in order. Come to think of it, it's been awhile since I was in a classy hotel so I guess I'm going to have to buy one. Jeez at one time when I was younger . . . I was in more hotel rooms than the Bible (and on more floors than linoleum) Maybe I can just get a black Yamika and fake it.

Planting flowers huh? That means I'm going to need a new manicure set . . . I hate dirt under my nails when I'm having a cocktail, so unbecoming of a mixed breed don't you think? Can't I just spread some seeds or something??? I'm afraid if I bend over, we'll either lose furniture or my gauze will end up a spaghetti strap . . . (please don't picture that . . . release before the trauma sets in)

Now I need something that can support a big boned guy such as myself . . . I was thinking a hammock made of the same stuff that they use to moor the Q E 2 with when she's in port? I hope the hell you have big trees or they'll be looking like weeping willows by the time I call it a night.

June . . . I was thinking it was in July . . . how silly of me.

Cheers!
Patsy Recline
(Patrick)

April 15, 2008
Subject: Something about a door closing and a
window opening . . .

Hi Guys,

My diagnosis of Ovarian Cancer came a week before my son's 13th birthday and a week and a half before my 46th birthday. My "moving ahead" meeting was today. It is 6 months later. Two days before Dan's 47th birthday. It has been an emotional, scary, wonderful, inspirational journey. I feel so alive and happy . . . this is a unique feeling that you cannot feel until you are faced with your own death. Perhaps this is when you get to the top of Maslow's hierarchy of needs into "self actualization". They are no guarantees in life. I move forward with hope, love and a renewed love of life. I remember again what Jake said to me "If they treat you for cancer – but then don't change anything in your life – why wouldn't it come back." Valid point! This book journals many changes in my life, which help me feel at least a moderate level of control.

When I started writing this book, it was based on the idea of writing letter's to Joshua. This idea came to be before I was diagnosed, and was an idea that would help me communicate important thoughts to Josh as he grew up thinking it would be easier for Josh to read what I had to say rather than talking about some things. As this book evolved, it became more about my journey. As this phase of the journey draws to an end, I realize something, in all the important things I wanted to tell Josh as he goes through adolescence, I realize now that what I have done, in these writings, I have told him all he needs to know. Not in the way that I expected. What I have told him is who I am, what is important to me and I think all the things he needs to grow into a wonderful adult. I hope this book has shown Josh to be positive, truly positive. I also hope he sees, it is the little things in life that make you happy – don't wait for someone to make you happy – you own your emotions, so you control your happiness. Be kind and patient because sympathy is important because empathy may come to you one day. Laugh and reach out to your friends, your family they are important. Do what brings you joy. Oh ya – be kind to the planet – it needs our help.

Throughout this journey Dan has been my strength, my shoulder to cry on, my source for laughter, my positive inspiration. I always thought of myself as a low maintenance girl . . . in some ways I am, but in many ways – in tough ways I am high maintenance – Dan was there for all my maintenance. He is my source.

My friends and family have been my catalyst, for writing, for staying positive and finally opening up and truly reaping the rewards of being vulnerable. It is truly a gift I have received and I will continue to receive.

This journey has been about family, faith, friends and community. I have found on this journey that my faith comes from within and from the bonds I have with my world. I have found that strength and solace comes with this faith. This lends itself to a positive attitude and brings me to happiness. Happiness is what it is all about.

How does this story end? Happy

Thanks,
Carole

PS By the way, my ribbon is teal blue.

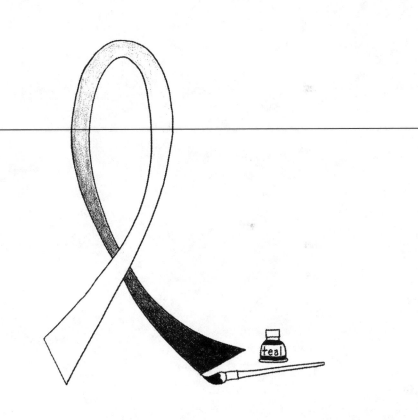

Epilogue

April 25, 2008
Subject: Withdrawal

Hi Guys,

Okay, I admit it. I am going through withdrawal and I don't think it's the drugs! I am so used to connecting with you guys whenever my mood is down or up or just whenever . . . so this was an interesting couple of weeks. After my final appointment (aside from 3 month check ups) last Tuesday, I had a wonderful day out golfing (in a cart) . . . the golf was so, so, the company was great and the weather was spectacular. When I got home that night I found out that my Dad had to go to emergency, with what turned out to be a minor stroke – but he is okay. Then on Saturday driving into the city to celebrate Dan's birthday a deer jumped out and smashed into our month old car! About $5,000 damage later all is well since Dan, Josh and I are not hurt. A friend of mine told me that an old Persian tradition was to sacrifice an animal whenever they got something new to keep the evil spirits out . . . they usually use a chicken – we used a deer!

After an eventful week last week, I looked forward to taking my last NSAID, (anti inflammatory for my day surgery last week) this past Monday. Tuesday morning my stomach felt awful, but as usual I got up and went for coffee. I had not missed a single coffee club in the entire 6 months of treatment . . . except when I was physically not in the village. After a few sips of coffee I had to get Dan to drive me home. My stomach was so sore. By 10:30 Dan had to drive me to Arnprior hospital. I was doubled over

in pain and Dan told the nurse how I had not once complained
during chemo . . . so this was serious. It was terrible. Pain
scale: 10 – constant. Aside from the pain my next worry was of
course . . . well my mind began to wonder. After giving me IV
painkillers and stuff to coat my stomach, around 5pm my pain was
under control. Thanks to Demerol and Gravol I was out for two
days on those. They gave me pills to coat my stomach and my own
decision to eat lots of yogurt for the good bacteria! (For those
at coffee club that heard nothing from me for two days, so sorry
about the worry I caused. I can tell you, if I had been on that
combo of drugs for my treatment, these mails and book would never
exist!) I was so zonked out.

Now that everything is back to normal, I felt a little sad this
morning . . . perhaps it is withdrawal from the Demerol . . .
or perhaps it is missing the connection with all of you. Either
way – I figure an occasional mail would be okay . . . I will have
to add a epilogue to the book!

Carole

May 26, 2008
Subject: moving

Hi Guys,

Once again I am compelled to write. Aside from venturing outside
Fitzroy Harbour with no wig on and, well, almost a two on the
shaver hairstyle . . . things are on the move. It is very funny
to notice that the most "cancer stares" I get are from babies.
There must be something about a woman with an almost baldhead
that attracts their attention. I find it quite amusing. I have
also noticed that people do seem to be very nice, returning carts
at stores for me etc.

As I begin to move on with my life, many things are changing.
First of all, I have found a Naturopath practitioner who is the
first person outside my family and friends that believe I can and
have beat my cancer. This is all new to me but I am finding it
wonderful just to have a support mechanism with someone who has
spent their life counseling people on natural remedies, feels that

I am on the right path with my diet, supplements and lifestyle changes. Regardless of anyone's belief in these things, I find it quite comforting, which is 80% of the battle right!

As I move into my life in remission, I am starting to do things that I hope will help others who are in my position. This week I am speaking at Mitel, as a cancer survivor (that seems surreal to me), to kick off Mitel's Campaign to raise money to support the Ottawa Hospital Foundation. This is nerve racking . . . speaking in front of my friends and co-workers! Well at least they tell you it is easier to speak in public when you know your topic . . . I guess I'm covered!

Other things are moving . . . today I packed and moved Ivan. As I have stated before, Ivan came into my life when I was first diagnosed and I knew she was leaving when I was done my treatment . . . I really didn't think the time would come so fast. Once you've had cancer – you notice and take note when time passes by quickly. It is a good reminder of everything you want to do, and how precious time is . . .

As always, I seem to find inspiration in Ivan . . . today I have noticed her collection of suitcases. Yes, suitcases. I must have moved at least 20 of them from the little yellow house by the river out to the U Haul, out of the U Haul and into the brown house down by another river . . . only thirty minutes away . . . ."It's not that far." "I will come and visit. I have to pick up my mail." I know we will see her. It will not be the same. Our little coffee club will miss her stories, her bright smile and infectious laugh. See here's why she will be missed. It's in the suitcases. Ivan's collection is made up of those old hard suitcases not much bigger than a computer bag or a carry on. Some of them are reminiscent of George Bailey's suitcase in "It's a wonderful life", the rest are those soft-sided flowered suitcases that many of us had when we were little girls and took with us on sleepovers to our friend's house. Some of them were packed with regular clothes, one was packed with clothes for her next trip on a tour to a festival in the Yukon, one was actually her overnight bag that she needs while in transition. Then there is the one that had all her special possessions in it . . . this is the most interesting. Aside from wondering what it contains, you have to actually stop and think. "Could I actually put all my special possessions in

one small suitcase?" This is a question that is quite apropos
today. As I have begun to edit my book and look back on the first
few pages, I notice that it is somewhat scattered, and dark . . .
it is nowhere near where my pages took me later in my journey.
As Ivan suggested "Call it Stage 1: Dark and Wandering". There
is definitely a transition that I have gone through as I fought
this battle. I have gone from dark and wandering . . . to today
noticing and more importantly understanding how, all that is
important to someone in the "material" world, can and should fit
into one suitcase.

Carole

May 28, 2008
Subject: Toastmasters

Hi Guys,

Well, I gave my "speech" at Mitel today at the kickoff. There
were about 100 people there. Some of which were my lunch buddies
that normally don't attend these things . . . so thanks for your
support guys . . . and you're welcome Pat (whose name I pulled
in a draw for $650 Ottawa Senators Hockey tickets!)
So Dianne (on this mailing) and I stood up and spoke about our
cancer experience. Dianne, whom had fought cancer 3 times now,
and is a two-year survivor, and I, felt we spoke well. People
commented to us that we did do well . . . as I pointed out to
her - whose going to tell us we sucked LOL . . . Dianne got
choked up and regained her composure and did great. I was in the
bathroom (nervous pee thing) and missed my name being called but
also regained my composure.

I wore my Fuck Cancer shirt. (Thanks Keleigh!) I covered the
"U" with a pink ribbon (couldn't find a teal ribbon) to make it
suitable for all audiences ;-) people loved the shirt and felt it
was appropriate for me to be wearing it, given my predisposition
to curse when things . . . well require a curse word!

So I am no Ivan, but they laughed when I expected them to laugh
and felt touched when expected.

I thought I would share a portion of what I said . . . namely my Top 5 reasons why Mitel Employees need to support the Ottawa Hospital Foundation campaign in buying new Chemo Chairs:

5. When your hair is falling out in clumps. There are way too many people to freak out by pulling your hair out in front of them, then to be wasting valuable practical joke time waiting at the cancer clinic for your treatment!
4. The Cancer clinic has 5 subscriptions to every magazine worth reading and there are never enough to go around. Nobody's going to donate money for magazines so a couple more chairs would help alleviate the waiting list on the good magazines.
3. With over 125 different forms of cancer . . . Hey I never knew what kind of "disease" the person sitting beside me had! And I really wanted to get out of there quick! On a more serious note . . .
2. Because until you or your loved one is faced with this disease - you cannot even begin to fathom how waiting even a day for a spot at the cancer clinic can be monumental. As they say we cannot buy time but buying a cancer chair quite literally is the next best thing!
1. Because they are predicting that the next generation . . . our children will face a 50% cancer rate . . . and until we can prevent cancer, the cancer chairs are only going to get busier.

My first attempt at being funny in a public forum like that!

Carole

June 12, 2008
Subject: Surviving Cancer is a full time job!

Hi Guys,

So, I am no closer to having my book edited . . . I have been filling my days with trying to be healthy including keeping my spirits high aka golfing, gardening, Josh's track meet, photography, girls' weekend at the cottage . . . you know the truly important things in life!

On top of that I have been trying to give back to my community (I am on the executive and working to bring some activities to Fitzroy to fill the hall and fill my heart . . . aka Latin dancing, more yoga and youth activities for my son . . . it seems that drinking events have somewhat fallen off the radar. I am also working for the Green Party, working on some advertisements and trying to organize them a little on setting up Policy and Procedures . . . aka trying to give back to the earth . . . which needs our help.

I am trying to give back and spread positivity . . . Unfortunately my cousin, whom I mentioned in an earlier mail, who fought Hodgkin's Lymphoma in her teens, then fought breast cancer recently has now been diagnosed with a melanoma. Fight hard Linda!!!! I also have been receiving requests from friends of my friends and relatives to send mail to others who have been stricken with cancer. This is part of my healing and payback!

Oh ya, I am trying to get back into the swing of things at work and am starting to look at work stuff (slowly . . . ;-)

I have been going to a Naturopathic Doctor since traditional medicine seems to stop when chemo is done. I am really finding it useful. But I finally got into see a Menopause doctor. Dr. Gamache . . . she is fabulous. She doesn't push medication and has a very holistic and natural approach to "treating" menopause symptoms. Aside from diet tips, fitness and vitamins, she also recommended sex (in any form LOL) 3 times a week to keep your muscles strong. Stop it! To help ward off incontinence later! By the way Dan loves Dr. Gamache LOL! I also went for my first mammogram. I was told not to wear deodorant. So I didn't. I asked the technician why no deodorant - thinking that they didn't want "gunk" on the expensive machine . . . however it is because the aluminum can effect it . . . so I am just thinking . . . what would all that aluminum do to us day after day, year after year . . . hummm - maybe the "hippies" who went braless, didn't shave and wore no deodorant had something right all those years ago.

For those who are local to Ottawa I have three things:

1. Next Friday June 20th at 7pm is my summer solstice party. BYOB (booze, bathing suit)
2. This Saturday in Fitzroy Harbour is a Wellness Fair organized by Sherri - one of my "Hi Guys" Ladies.

3. Ivan is performing this Saturday June 14th at 11:30 am at West Fest, at the Main Stage.

June 21, 2008
Subject: Summer is here!

Hi Guys,

Thanks to everyone who came to celebrate the summer solstice last night. It was fabulous, speaking of which, Patrick looked Fabulous in his yellow gauze aka Mother Nature attire, as well as Sonya's Wiccan garb and Diane's pagan princess outfit! (Pictures will be posted on Facebook)

As I planned for the planting of a flower, pre-requisite for admission to the party, as a symbol and reminder of my friends, I realized my garden is full! Yes, both literally and figuratively. Flowers had to be planted in a new garden.

Last night marked 6 months since the darkest day . . . yes both literally and figuratively, in that I had my hysterectomy Dec 21st the winter equinox!

What a wonderful way to mark the end of my cancer story. I have been procrastinating in editing my book. Today I have the logical conclusion to my journey.

For those who attended I hope the sunflower seedling (a symbol for Ovarian Cancer) I gave you grows high and proud, producing plenty of seeds — perhaps we will celebrate the harvest of the seeds. What? Another party with the girls — sounds like a plan. Maybe it will coincide with a book publishing party! For those who couldn't make it, I will plant a flower today and will be thinking of you.

As I lay in my hammock typing this on my blackberry enjoying my backyard, writing to my friends I find serenity and hope for the future!

I love all of you for providing me strength and laughter!

Thank you.
Carole

Meet my 'Hi Guys'

Hi Guys,

Since this list contains, friends in Fitzroy, work friends, old school buddies, and family there are many of you who have never met. While most of you live in Ottawa, I there are people from across Canada, the US, England. So, with that in mind, meet my guys!

Angie – My "little" sister. Yes, the one that my brother Pat and I turkey tied, gagged and stuffed in the closet and went down for Sunday dinner. The same one that got a little tipsy one night and actually had a Chinese noodle laugh out her nose! My only sister, the one that I was with in England and we nearly peed my pants laughing so hard, walking home from a pub with my cousin Viv. The one who just discovered she is a good runner after all these years being the "princess" of the family and is now a jock! The one that I look forward to years of getting closer to and appreciating – just like mom said we would.

Ann – My American friend – wife of Dan's "Marine coaching" friend Al. Ann is one of these truly nice people, who is always thinking of other people. This is probably why she worked at the American Embassy in Ottawa . . . and someone whom I haven't seen in about 20 years. She and her husband are the reason why we drove 12 hours to Virginia for a weekend. Just to see Al graduate from University! She is one of the few female friends whom is an avid football fan . . . perhaps even more than me. She is a breast cancer survivor.

Annette – not just a friend in Fitzroy Harbour, she was a caregiver for Josh. With Annette there is always a wonderful conversation always a laugh and a singing voice that is captivating. I can particularly remember a rendition of Blue Bayou in my living room on a Scavenger Hunt night . . . she is the 'subject' in one of my favorite pictures ever I took at our Halloween costume party, when she was dressed as a hippie. Her mom has cancer.

Beryl – my mom. Not just a wonderful mom, she is one of the funniest people I know. She is one of those people that everyone is attracted to . . . she is a storyteller, whether she knows it or not she made me a strong, independent woman. She travelled the world and I was enthralled by the exciting life. Living in Russia and Germany in the 50's with stories of her standing on her rooftop in England during the war with her sister and brother . . . looking at the black specs dropping from the plane and then realizing they were bombs and scurrying down to the basement for shelter. But my favorite story is more recent and I really must share it with you. My mom and Dad were spending the winter in Arizona. My Uncle Bill was over from England visiting. The three of them set off on a tour on one of those 20 seater buses. My mother was busily chatting with my Uncle. She noticed a daughter, mom and "a little old lady" (her words – but my mom was about 75 at the time!) all chatting in Spanish seated on the other side of her. As she continued to chat, without looking she grabbed the seat belt to try to do it up. As she continued to talk and try to do up her seat belt she heard the "little old lady" getting louder and louder saying something in Spanish. Feeling that the woman's voice had gone beyond a respectable "on the bus" volume she turned around to find out what was wrong with this woman. As she turned her head to the lady, she looked down, saw the old ladies foot in her hand, which she had been yanking on for a few minutes to try to insert it into her seat belt!

Buzz (Frank) – my dad. A great Dad! Thanks to Dad, for all the weekends camping, touring around to various provincial parks, for teaching me how to golf, "making me" watch golf and instilling a love of football in me, teaching me how to play poker, a love of westerns and war movies, teaching me about recycling before it was "green". Thanks for intriguing me with your "spy" stories, for bringing home Letraset, consisting of MIG bombers, nuclear explosions and tanks on it. Walking in the door with a briefcase handcuffed to your wrist, walking through customs at the airport with a flip of your passport . . . making me intrigued with spy stories and helped fuel my curiosity. He beat prostate cancer.

Carol – a Fitzroy friend, baseball buddy, member of my all ladies investment club, designer of my opal and diamond family ring, and always a trendsetter in fashion which is perfectly juxtaposed against her dressed as one of my favorite costumes at one of our Halloween parties, her dressed as Mimi off Drew Carey.

Cathy – a Fitzroy friend, 20 years of fun, great conversations and laughter . . . Cathy's! I know, no matter how badly I deliver a joke . . . I can make her laugh! She is always available on-line, ready to help me through menopause questions. She is there to help find something on the internet, or just there to bounce things off of. House boating, Cuba, camping, darts, LCBO dinners, golf weekend trips, Cathy is always up for a party and up for some fun.

Cheryl – a Fitzroy friend, a nurse and the inspiration for my "no flu for you" email last fall and someone who manages to live and sleep next to the loudest snorer ever, who almost allowed us sent him out onto the lake on a rubber raft one group camping trip to somehow get rid of the snoring.

Chris – a friend, softball and golf buddy, whose thoughts and emails have been a great inspiration. One night at softball, Chris and I were outside discussing something important I am sure, when we saw a meteorite. Not a falling star but an actual meteorite with a glowing blue tail. That was a once in a lifetime opportunity.

Dave – my work friend, lunch buddy and Spring Opener golf partner. Dave was one of my work buddies on the road trip from Phoenix to Vegas. Dave's crude sense of humor makes me laugh and spurs me on to match his. Dave was the guy who said, "With a guy, any conversation is two steps from a conversation about a blow job" (sorry to some . . .)

Debbie D – a Fitzroy friend and weekend coffee club member. A quiet friend or so we thought, until two years ago at our group camping weekend, who showed why she fits in with the Fitzroy crowd when she came out of her shell!

Debbie R — a Fitzroy friend — I am pretty sure Deb was my coach on some of those" training sessions" that helped me handle the alcohol in the chemo! Someone who always makes you laugh.

Dianne H — a work friend, my HR representatives for years and my pillar through all of this. Dianne is a two-year cancer survivor . . . whose experience has helped me through this with first hand experience. Dianne and I were golfing at a work tournament on a cold and blustery day in October and thought it would be discourteous to turn town the "tequila rose coloured jiggers" we were offered and ended up in our golf cart half way up a hill stuck and the cart half tipped over.

Dianne L — Dianne is one of my first friends in Fitzroy. She is also a back catcher, who has webbed toes, and is a former lifeguard too. There have been many laughs with Dianne. Some of the best were our laughs on the houseboat we rented one summer. Or perhaps it was laughing at James, when we had the mixed lingerie party. Tough call! Her husband had cancer and her son died breast cancer.

Doug — a work friend, former boss, former Tae Kwan Do partner and current peer at work! Doug is the person who always seems to know the answer. From how our 'stock options work' to explaining what an ASIC, an FPGA is, and was my mentor and teacher of all things technical at work. He is always there for me to explain how things work in a way that I can understand. Doug's wife is a breast cancer survivor.

Gwen — a Fitzroy friend and golf partner. Gwen is just funny. One Wednesday, golfing with our regular group, Noella, my mother in law joined our group. When we got home, I heard Noella talking to Dan in the Kitchen, "Does Carole always pee in the bunker?" WHAT, I scurried into the kitchen. Noella explained that my friend Gwen told her that on the 4th whole, when I bent down in the bunker (to avoid getting hit by an errant ball) Gwen told her I was peeing in the bunker. I dialed Gwen immediately and all I could hear was laughing on the end of the phone. Of course when I hung up I did have to ask why Noella actually thought I would pee in a bunker . . . .

Heather — my sister in law, Dan's little brother Lee's wife. She is a strong fun loving woman. It has been my pleasure watching her grow in confidence over the 15 years I have known her. My favorite story is about us being in the hot tub one night, her and I happening across a partially clothed drunk person, in mid February, standing in my laneway and ensuring he got home safe . . . that's perhaps another story for another day! Her Dad has cancer.

Ivan – a Fitzroy friend, coffee club member, a storyteller with interesting stories of things I have never done, people I will never meet. Now that I write this . . . perhaps she reminds me of my mom . . . .

Jack & Bev – Uncle Jack and Auntie Bev. Crazy Jack as Dad used to call him. As I got older and heard about his stories and some of his jokes, perhaps he is crazy Jack. With 5 kids and Jack, Bev is one patient woman! They are the parents of my cousin Linda, who had fought cancer twice and is on this list!

Jane – a swimming friend. Jane is a dynamo, an inspiration for being an athlete as we age. She is one of a group of phenomenal people I just met two years ago. Jane inspires me to swim harder, go longer and inspired me to buy a bike in preparation for a triathlon. We'll have to see about that one.

Jill – a friend from high school, I recall going to a dance with Jill and Mary. I was wearing a new salmon coloured raincoat that I just loved. I "borrowed" some vodka from home and a can of frozen orange juice, which was to be our pre-dance drinks. Somehow the orange juice spilled all over my new coat. It was never the same but we had a great time at the dance. We get together several times a year. Jill is definitely someone that I wish I knew better earlier. We get together with a group of friends from high school and it seems that every time we get together, we have great conversations and become closer. I am so glad.

Jodie – a new football friend. Her husband coaches with Dan for Josh's team. Jodie is a teacher, with 4 kids under 13 and organizes, buys the food, sets up, cooks and sells food for the football team's canteen at games . . . oh ya and was the manager of the team . . . and I have never seen her not smile. Need I say more?

Judy B – Judy is one of those people that I like to bounce problems off of, she is that person that is dependable, smart and oh ya . . . the root of all those practical jokes that everybody blames on her husband Ken. They are her ideas, gets Ken to carry out the prank, and silently laughs while we all blame Ken. We know it was Judy whose idea it was to put all the pine cones in our car filling it up so high that we couldn't fit our legs in, we know it was you who put the raw egg on our ceiling fan one Halloween party, we know it was you, so many times . . . thanks for the fun! (Did you like the bushel of apples in your bed? ;-)

Judy W – a Fitzroy friend, a member of my all female investment club, a neighbor. Judy is responsible for helping us become part of the community. She invited us to go to Montebello with a gang from the village. We met and became friends with many people on that first trip and enjoyed many other trips there. Judy was one of my first golf buddies. We played softball together. My favorite memory was cruising up and down the Rideau Canal in her beautifully restored wooden boat, eating homemade antipasto and drinking red wine.

Karen – is a Fitzroy friend, a softball friend and a pillar in our community. Karen is an inspiration for me, as she has overcome many trials and tribulations after waking up one New Years Day somehow contracting a virus that perplexed doctors and left her paralyzed down one side. Karen walks without feeling in her leg but she doesn't let anything keep her down. She is one of my heroes.

Kay – a golf buddy. Kay has a sense of humor that sneaks up on you . . . my favorite laugh with her is hearing her trying to find someone in the crowd of twenty of us golfing for a weekend getaway, to back her up that there really existed in a commercial from her childhood about Stoopy Doop the safety dog, and then trying hard to convince us that she didn't imagine this character . . . anybody heard of Stoopy Doop???

Kristen – an old girl guide friend, a Nepean Sportsplex swimming buddy and high school friend. We have so many high school stories . . . but the one I can think of, is about skipping out of our geography class on the last day of Grade 12 to start celebrating early . . . but I won't tell that story since Kristin is a respected lawyer now! Her dad has prostate cancer.

Laurie – a Fitzroy friend, a coffee club member – she always has a funny story, is quick to laugh but I always remember her telling the story about when she walked into the police station on Carp Road, covered in blood and telling the officer, "I've been in a car accident." when Laurie saw their panicked looks, she quickly added that "No, this isn't my blood – I hit a deer and my window was open and its the deer's blood. I just need something to wipe the blood off!"

Linda – my cousin – Linda is two years older than me. When I took the train to visit Cathy and Nancy – her twin sisters who were my age, I remember thinking how cool she was. We ended up at a record store in London, Ont. and she prompted me to buy a huge poster with the "Best Guitarist" (This is significant because it helped cement my "coolness" with Dan a few years later.) Linda was an Iggy Pop fan . . . which started me on my way to listening to punk myself (Also helping solidify my "coolness" with Dan) Linda was my first encounter with Cancer. Shortly after that summer trip to London, Linda developed Hodgkin's Disease. Linda is now close to 50, a long time cancer survivor and more recently a breast cancer survivor.

Mary – my oldest friend – Mary and I met when we were in grade 2. Mary and I have grown up together. We both got our first ever purses in grade 2, in grade 5 her speech was about her and I being witches, after practicing incantations in my room and casting love spells on our would be boyfriends, we shared our first bottle of Country Roads Apple Wine prior to our first dance in high school. Mary and I walked to school together, both grade school and high school. Every morning for 11 years we walked together! We studied together, we discussed boyfriends and I remember a date, she was so nervous she asked me what to drink to calm down. I told her "a Manhattan . . . it's strong," I guess she really didn't know how strong – but I am told the date was not a success as she decided she needed more than one.

Maureen – a work friend – Maureen and I have been working together for about 22 years. We have grown up together in the work place. Both of us changing our roles, evolving and growing! But my favorite story of Maureen is years ago we went on a work ski trip. If you look real hard at Dan's forehead you can see a little tiny scar, where Maureen threw a coaster at him from across the bar!

MJ – a Fitzroy friend, golf buddy, private nurse! MJ is always sticking needles in me, first it was injecting hormones – we'll give her an assist in creating Josh! MJ did everything when we had to bury Josh's twin, Matthew. Most recently she was helping me get my allergy shots. MJ brought me to the Madawaska golf course as on a "Bring a Friend" night . . . I joined the next year and have been golfing ever since. But MJ is of course renowned for her charade playing – yes MJ created the oversize both arms extended clapping together more like an alligator than a stapler motion – bringing joy to all who were there to witness it and joy to some who have only seen it second hand.

Noella – my Mother in law. Dan always jokes about his mom loving me more than him. We know this is not true, but I have known her for 27 years. We have had laughs, great conversations, and wonderful moments together beyond your typical family get-togethers. Does she love me more than Dan? No, but I have always felt loved by her, perhaps like the daughter she never had. Several of her sisters had cancer.

Pam – a Fitzroy friend, an occasional coffee club member . . . I remember her telling us about being a young woman in training to be a nurse in England and something about working with the Royal Navy and her confusion over "seamen" ejaculating from the plane instead of ejecting . . . you have to hear her tell it!

Pat D – a work friend, lunch buddy, golf buddy. Lunch time is always a learning experience about men and women and how they think. It is always a laugh, and fun to hear different perspectives. How else would I keep up with hockey?

Patricia I – work friend – Pat was our work mom. Pat is the person who kept all those engineers in line, she was there for those who need support, she is there to help sort out. Pat is now retired and we miss her.

Patrick – a Fitzroy friend – Well if you have been following along on these emails since the beginning you will agree with me that Patrick is fabulous in more ways than one! Patrick and his partner Tim can tell you that our small village of Fitzroy is much more tolerant than one might expect! What a wonderful sense of humor. Patrick is the only male ever invited to my

summer solstice and we hope to see him this year in a white
gauze dress!

Patti – a work friend – now just a friend! Patti and I literally
worked side by side for 20 years. The laughs we shared along the
way were just too many to mention and probably just not funny to
anyone that wasn't there, working with us. I do recall a few things
that Patti taught me. The first took years and years. Patti and I
had many arguments over lunch. People around us thought we weren't
friends because we were often in heated arguments – probably about
abortion or some other hot topic of the day. What I learned from
Patti is that you can discuss hot topics, remain friends and that
it is stimulating to challenge your beliefs. This can be fun if you
know that whom you were discussing these issues with respected you
and you respected them and that one differing opinion on one topic
doesn't mean you can't be friends. The other thing about Patti is
that I one day at lunch, I asked her to tell me what a common friend
had told her. She refused. I was a bit perplexed, as we were so
close. She had to share it with me! Didn't she? She explained that
this other friend had told her the information in confidence. At
first I was dumbfounded. This is not the "code of sisterhood." You
always tell your better friend what the other friend said . . . at
least that is what I had learned from past experiences . . . much
to my chagrin . . . until that day. From that point on I knew I
could trust Patti with anything. This is a strong lesson and this
is a value that I have adopted. Her mother died of lung cancer.

Peggy – a Fitzroy friend, golf buddy – Peggy is one of our organizers
and my oldest friend – not how long I've known her . . . she's
just the oldest! She organizes golf trips, shopping outings and
countless other events. She is often heard complaining about "the
Fitzroy people drinking too much . . . and yet she keeps organizing
activities for us . . . hummm. My funniest story is when Gord and
Peggy, Dan and I were in Myrtle Beach for a week of golf. Peggy
hit a put. It hit the hole and it popped out. "Ahhh," we said, but
then it happened again and again. We started to laugh and Peggy
got annoyed. Then it happened two more times – each time hitting
the hole and popping out. She also started to laugh. The funniest
part – she had to score an 8, on a mini putt hole!

Ralph – work friend, golf buddy, someone whom I can close the
door to his office and rant! Someone whom which I can have an

occasional discussion on philosophy. I remember a work golf event where I took Ralph's blackberry and told him I sent an email to our VP. The panicked look on his face was priceless when what I had done was that I actually emailed one of the other people out on the golf course.

Sally – a Fitzroy friend, the owner of the cottage whom we so dearly love to have our girls weekend . . . every time with Sally is a laugh. Sally laughs the loudest and cries the hardest. I could not tell Sally about my cancer I had to get MJ to tell her, as I knew she would not take it well. Sally is a kind, warm soul.

Sandra – a Fitzroy friend – the only person I know who chases her rye with vodka . . . my favorite laugh – Sandra trying to take out her contact lenses at 4 in the morning after chasing her rye with vodka one family camping weekend.

Sandy – a work friend – My old smoking buddy! Oh there was so much to learn out in that smoking area. A few laughs but I think it was more of a support group helping each other figure out the rat race.

Sarah M – a work friend in our Wales office, I see her several times a year. My favorite story is when we were in Paris together. After 12 years of French in school, I asked our cab driver for une recette, the cab driver stared at me, and Sarah, with only 1 year of French in University and 1 year living in France, spoke better French than me, asked the cab driver for un recu. Apparently I had asked for a recipe, Sarah had asked for the receipt.

Sarah W – a work friend out of the U.S. – Sarah and I shared a great night in Palm Springs, talking about music; punk and other . . . She was a fast friend, very interesting and captivating. We maybe have talked about 5 times in our lives until recently. I thought about her this summer when the bridge collapsed in Minneapolis. We just re-connected after she changed jobs. Her husband had cancer.

Sean – my brother in law – Sean is funny, and very sweet. Sean lived with us when Dan and I first got married. If anyone has heard Dan and I refer to each other as booby, bobby-do, Bob or any derivative there of, it is due to Sean. Sean gave us those nicknames and they stuck!

Sharon – a Fitzroy friend – Sharon and I met through our sons. It was a treat to learn how similar we were. With both of us growing up in the same area of Ottawa, similar tastes in music, similar tastes in movies and similar experiences as we were growing up.

Sherri W – a Fitzroy friend who is just one of those good-natured people, always a smile and a laugh! Aside from her wonderful dips at the craft fair, raising money for breast cancer (I get my Thing-me-boobs key chains from her) my 'fondest' memory of Sherri, is standing outside last December burning a magazine with scary, disheartening cancer stats in it . . . very therapeutic!!!!

Sherry K – a Fitzroy friend, a coffee club member, Sherry is strong, competitive, a great athlete and underneath all of that is a sweet, sensitive woman whom she occasionally lets us see!

Sonya – a Fitzroy friend, coffee club member, only on the weekends now, and Josh's second mom – There are so many laughs where do you start? Another organizer, a great caregiver, an artist and crafts person, a kind soul who has just retired her 'caregiver' business and started a new life out in the workforce. My fondest memory is just a few weeks ago, when we went shopping and I could see a whole new strength, after her husband just recovered from a stroke. Sonya is the person who illustrated the cover of this book and all the illustrations inside! Her mom had cancer

Sue C – my next-door neighbor when growing up. Sue is such a kind person. She is helpful. She was closest to my little sister but I remember playing outside in our yards hide and seek, tag and skipping. We see each other about once a year now on Boxing Day. I love hearing her stories as she travels to Major League Ball Parks across the US, ticking them off until they are all done.

Sue H – a Fitzroy friend, softball buddy – Years ago, one morning – perhaps when I was on maternity leave, I noticed a bat sleeping on the pillow in my TV room. Sue came over to help out. Both of us were freaked out about the bat, neither of us had the courage to get rid of it. Sue called her husband Brent to come over and get rid of the bat for us. We waited in anticipation for Brent to come and 'rescue' us. When he arrived, he laughed and asked us "Did we not notice that the bat had not moved at all?" Well neither of us got any closer than about 5 feet away and then quickly backed out of the room. Brent quickly scooped up the bad which was dead . . . I guess my cat had brought it to me as a present . . . well it was still scary to us.

Steve - work friend, lunch buddy, golf friend - another person I have worked with for years, another example of how you can have differing opinions, discuss it, argue and still stay friends, (he'll be mad that I gave this away . . . but he's a big huge Teddy Bear.) There are many funny stories, how many "Spring Openers" golf days have I been too? There's one about a long cab ride from Calabogie Highlands Golf Course but again . . . some stories you just have to be there.

Tammy - a Fitzroy friend - I remember having a great time and getting to know Tammy at Ursula's LCBO "drink" party. I didn't really know Tammy too well before this party and it was great to discover a friendship!

Ted & Mae - Dan's Uncle Ted - a big, huge man, a retired professional hockey player in the WHA, whose real claim to fame, was that he was an extra in the movie Slap Shot and got to "check" Paul Newman!. Last year when we went to Arizona, we had a wonderful time, especially one night playing a Neil Diamond DVD that ended up with Ted, Aunt Mae, Noella, Josh, Dan and I all dancing and singing to Neil in their living room. Their daughter Debbie, around my age, died of breast cancer several years ago.

Tim - A Fitzroy Friend - Tim is the perfect balance for Patrick. The quiet one! The shy one! We're not really sure, but we think he spent the most money on a Halloween costume for our party . . . and effort, ordering a Black Spiderman Lycra outfit from China for our Halloween party last year. This is the shy one . . . wait a minute . . . did I not see a picture of Tim on Facebook wearing a long red wig, shirt undone, swinging on a brass pole? And Tim doesn't drink!

Vicky - a Fitzroy Friend and golf buddy. Hummm which is my funniest thought of Vicky . . . My favorite time golfing was with Vicky and MJ in the club championship and seeing Vicky stand up in the covered golf cart pretending to be Napoleon, (yes, she is that short) wait, no, it was last summer when she was 'sleeping' on the couch at Sally's cottage and Gwen and I manipulated her arms to act out her charades – since it was her turn and we didn't want her to miss it . . . then suddenly, she woke up saw her arm in the air and was shocked to see it. Of course I have to admit – I love that she "loves" my golf swing . . . and sometimes she makes me smile inside – when I am not quite decompressed from my work day and zoned into fun time/golf mode.

Vivienne – my cousin who lives in England – I first met Viv when I was 12 and she was 22. Even back then, I really felt a connection despite the age discrepancy. Since that first meeting we have been together 5 times over 20 odd years. Viv is a kindred spirit. We are so very close. Every time we get together conversations flows, and we just get along. My mom always wondered about nature vs nurture, as I was adopted. Well I think the connection with Viv is a strong argument for nurture since Viv's mom and my mom are sisters, we were certainly raised by very similar women.

Zena – a brand new friend who lives in Vancouver – she is a brilliant young businesswoman, who is also working on her PhD and is partner to Ivan. I can't wait to get to know Zena better . . . apparently she hosts a Halloween party that rivals the one Dan and I host. And seeing how I dressed as "Xena, warrior goddess" for Halloween one year how can I not like a woman like that!

I have mentioned a few of my friends that I know have had direct connections to cancer, but I know the all of the people on this list have been touched by cancer (besides me . . . .)

Thanks you "Guys"!